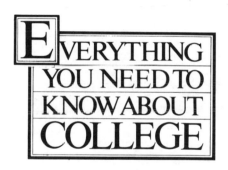

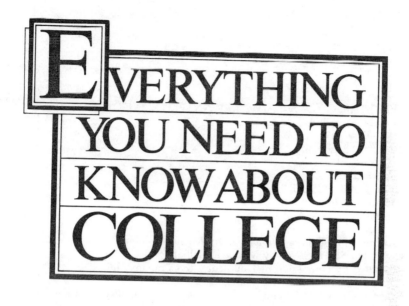

EVERYTHING YOU NEED TO KNOW ABOUT COLLEGE

Andre Bustanoby

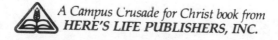
A Campus Crusade for Christ book from
HERE'S LIFE PUBLISHERS, INC.

EVERYTHING YOU'VE ALWAYS WANTED (NEEDED)
TO KNOW ABOUT COLLEGE

By Andre Bustanoby

Published by
HERE'S LIFE PUBLISHERS, INC.
P.O. Box 1576
San Bernardino, CA 92402

Library of Congress Catalogue Card 82-084553
ISBN 0-89840-034-1
HLP Product No. 95-040-2

Printed in the United States of America.

CONTENTS

CHAPTER ONE
So You're Going To College!

You've decided on college...or you are helping someone else make that decision. Great! You've made a wise move. A college education can help you (or your friend) in many ways: intellectually, socially, and, of course, vocationally. It can provide a chance to meet new people, make new friends and mature as a person. It can stimulate you to think, to learn, to develop your mind. It can teach you marketable skills and improve your chances of landing a good job when you graduate.

U.S. Bureau of Labor statistics reveal that, during one recession, the unemployment ratio was only 1.5% for college graduates (for high school grads it was 4.5%; 8.5% for those who never finished high school. Of course, a college education doesn't guarantee success; you still must show competence on the job! But college is a good place to start.

This book is designed to help the Christian student—and those who advise him—with his decisions about entering a secular college. If you are a high school student, this book will help you learn what college is and how it works. It will give you guidelines for selecting a college, for entering it, and for paying for it. We will also explore some of the circumstances you can expect when you move away from home and into the new environment of campus living.

If you are a college freshman, this book will help you as you adapt to life in the dormitory, fraternity or sorority. It will give you pointers on relating to both Christians and non-Christians on campus. It will inform you about some of the many different philosophies and moral and spiritual pressures you will encounter.

CHAPTER TWO
College: What Is It And
How Does It Work?

Though you've already decided to go to college, you might need a clearer idea of its role and how it works. I think most of us agree that college is desirable for the interested and academically qualified student, but let's review some of the basics and nail down some of the terms used.

All education above high school is called "higher education." Sometimes it's called "post-secondary education." College is seen not only as the center of a community's intellectual life, but also the seat of training of leaders for public and professional life.

HIGHER EDUCATION INSTITUTIONS

Institutions of "higher education" include universities, four-year colleges, separately organized professional schools and junior colleges.

Junior College. The junior college, often called a "community college," offers a two-year program of study. Junior college courses fall into two categories: transfer programs and vocational-technical programs. The transfer program is comparable to the first two years of a four-year liberal arts college. It prepares the student to enter a four-year college at the junior year level.

The vocational-technical programs are designed to prepare students for careers below the technical level that more advanced programs attempt to reach. Some examples would be electronics, metal-working and office machine operation.

Completion of either a transfer or a vocational program

leads to the award of an associate's degree — usually an Associate in Arts (A.A.) or Associate in Science (A.S.).

The community college program is uniquely American and has much to commend itself to the student and to those advising him on higher education. Many community colleges offer quality education and have arrangements for the transfer of credits when the student matriculates (enrolls in) the state four-year college. If your community college has such a program, it will be discussed in detail in the school catalogue. *Be sure* you understand the requirements for transfer of credit if you choose to go this route. Don't enroll under a false assumption and find out later that you can't transfer your credits to a four-year college.

One advantage to attending a community college before attending a four-year school is financial. Often the cost of education is less than it is in the four-year college. Here in Maryland we have several community colleges that have transfer agreements with the University of Maryland at College Park. The typical cost for community college in tuition and fees per year is $397, while at the University of Maryland the cost is $1072. This means that the first two years of education at a community college is $1350 less expensive than at the University of Maryland. Given a transfer advantage, the student saves a tidy sum.

Another advantage is that the student can live at home and commute to the community college. Considering current food and housing costs, such a prospect is attractive. However both the parents and the student should be aware of the possibility of other problems with this arrangement. Any time an adult child lives at home there is a risk of friction between parent and child.

A third advantage of attending a community college is something called "cultural continuity." This simply means that the environment in which the student studies, lives and works is the same as it was in his high school days. The pressure of college study and work may be all some students can handle at one time. They might experience problems with cultural adjustment in a school where the environment differs significantly from what they were used to at home. They may need this cultural continuity to succeed in college.[1]

College. A college usually offers a four-year program leading to a bachelor's degree such as Bachelor of Arts (B.A.) or Bachelor of Science (B.S.). The type of bachelor's degree indicates your major or the emphasis of your study in the last two years. A B.A. would indicate a major in the arts; a B.S. indicates a major in the sciences. There are other types of bachelor degrees as well.

The student's major is not declared until after the first two years of college. Many students entering college get themselves worked up unnecessarily because they don't know what kind of a career they want. Such fretting is unnecessary.

The purpose of a four-year education is not to prepare you for a career. It is designed to develop your God-given intellect so you can become creative even as He is creative. Certainly your creativeness will not be in the same magnitude, but as creatures made in the image of God, we were designed to be the masters and rulers of His creation (Genesis 1:28).

Consequently, the first two years are designed to give you a broad exposure to a variety of interests, in both the arts and the sciences. Extracurricular activities also often help you get in touch with your talents and interests. You will find your interests develop in a particular direction as time goes by.

For example, I went to Nyack College in New York with a view to going to seminary—a professional graduate school. I wanted to become a pastor. I received a Bachelor of Science (B.S.) from Nyack, and then a Master of Theology (Th.M.) from Dallas Theological Seminary in Texas. My education was broad enough to enable me to communicate both in the spoken and written word. During the next thirteen years I preached, taught college and seminary, and wrote articles in the field of Bible and theology.

Seeing a need for more skill in counseling, I went for a

Master of Arts in Marriage and Family Therapy at Azusa Pacific College in California. This enabled me to move to a field related to the pastoral ministry. I have been in the private practice of marriage and family therapy since 1973 and am currently the president of my professional organization in Maryland. Since 1973 I have written several books in the field of marriage and the family. I have continued with my teaching skills both at the college and seminary level.

My point is this. Don't fret about a career. Because of the longevity of Americans today, you're liable to have several careers before you meet the Lord. Get an education to expand your mind and experience. Your careers will come as a matter of course.

Now let's get back to the college program. The four-year course is normally broken into fall and spring semesters (with a summer break) or into trimesters that cover fall, spring and summer terms with brief breaks between them.

In a liberal arts course, students normally take four or five subjects each term. For each weekly hour of classwork over the semester, one unit of credit is given. For example, if you have a two-hour or two-credit course, that course meets two hours a week for the semester in which you get your two credits. Laboratory courses usually require two or three hours in the lab for each unit of credit. A normal program includes 15 or 16 hours of class a week.

Some colleges allow students to begin professional studies in their junior or senior year and grant a bachelor's degree after the first, second or third year of professional school. This is common with law, medical and engineering studies.

University. The university usually includes an undergraduate college, a graduate division (awarding master's and doctor's degrees) and one or more professional schools (law, medicine, engineering). Although they enroll large numbers of undergraduate students (students working at the bachelor's level), universities tend to emphasize graduate instruction and research with an eye to master's degrees and doctorates.

A Master of Arts Degree (M.A.) is sometimes given upon

the completion of a fifth year of work. That fifth year is often a full year of work—fall, spring and summer. There was a time when a bachelor's degree was something special. Today it is becoming as common as a high school diploma, and the master's degree is more and more becoming the norm for the educated American. I don't mean to imply by this that education merely confers status. You will learn that an advanced degree does not excuse incompetence.

This book does not discuss graduate or professional programs, but as you proceed with your education you will want to become more aware of what is available in graduate studies. This is especially important as you begin to focus on your field of interest.

Professional School. I only mention professional schools to complete the picture of "higher education." These schools accept only those students who have a bachelor's degree. Such schools train men and women in the fields of technology, medicine and theology. Seminary is technically a professional school. It is possible for a person to become a minister in some denominations with neither college nor seminary, but I recommend both.

Federal Institutions. To round out the picture of higher education, I should say something about federal institutions. The federal government is involved in higher education, both at the undergraduate and graduate levels. The better-known undergraduate schools are the service academies: The Military Academy at West Point, N.Y.; the Naval Academy at Annapolis, Md; and the Air Force Academy at Colorado Springs, Colo. These schools combine undergraduate, college-level education with officer training.

Lesser-known undergraduate officer academies are the Coast Guard Academy at New London, Conn. (run by the Treasury Department) and the Merchant Marine Academy at Kings Point, N.Y. (run by the Department of Commerce). Other specialized federal institutions are the Naval War College, Naval Post-graduate School, Army War College and the Air University. All of these offer advanced study for military officers.

The Department of Agriculture runs a graduate school in Washington, D.C. It enrolls more that 5,000 students but awards no degree.

SPECIAL PROGRAMS

The stereotyped concept of college is composed of classrooms, lectures, laboratories and exams. By going through the process, you rack up credits toward a degree. But you should be aware that college today offers a wider educational experience than that. Here are some special programs you should be aware of.

Advanced Placement of Freshmen. Some high schools offer study in advanced subjects to the brighter students. This work may be credited toward a student's college degree if he passes qualifying tests.

Let's say that the student is accepted by a college that subscribes to this program. He may take a three-hour exam in the spring prior to his matriculation to college. The college decides if the student will receive college credit and be permitted to go on to a more advanced course.

Work-Study Plans. This plan permits the student to alternate periods of several weeks in the classroom and on the job. This plan initiated by the School of Engineering at the University of Cincinnati paired students who alternated between their place of employment and the classroom. Other well-known institutions using this program include Northeastern University, Antioch College, Fenn College, and The Rochester Institute of Technology.

The Reserve Officer Training Corps (ROTC). The Army, Navy and Air Force are represented in many institutions through the ROTC program, which produces a large number of career officers. This two- to four-year program is voluntary on most campuses.

The Air Force and Navy offer two, three and four-year scholarship programs. The Army offers a four-year scholarship program. Non-scholarship cadets in the Army's Advanced Course (final two years) receives the same allowances as scholarship holders over the last two years.

Undergraduate Study Abroad. Well over 100 institutions participate in this program. Students can spend anywhere from a semester to an academic year at a university in another country. The Council on International Education Exchange (CIEE) sponsors overseas programs in France, Russia, Japan and Spain.[2] For more information on these and other CIEE programs write:

Council on International Education Exchange
777 United Nations Plaza
New York, NY 10017

Extension and Correspondence Courses. Those who are unable to attend college full time find this a helpful program. Extensions work is generally taken by part-time students at off-campus centers. If you are not yet ready to attend college full time, a correspondence course may help you get started. These are also excellent options for the student who may have to drop out of school.

Men in the armed forces will want to investigate correspondence opportunities. For years the United States Armed Forces Institute (USAFI) has given college-bound servicemen an opportunity to get a head start by offering college credit for correspondence courses taken through USAFI.

New Forms of Higher Education. Here are some less traditional approaches to higher education:[3]

1. Getting a degree without attending college. This is called an external degree. See Chapter Four for more on this.

2. Exchanging learning. The exchange doesn't do the teaching, but puts teachers and students in touch with each other.

3. Free universities. These are similar to learning exchanges. But they go further than just maintaining a list of teachers. They will print a catalogue and may charge a registration fee.

4. The campus-free college. This is a network of program

advisors throughout the country with an office in
Washington, D.C. Students get together with a program advisor and put together learning packages based in their own
communities. You really have to be a self-starter to use a
program such as this.

ADMINISTRATIVE STRUCTURE OF THE COLLEGE

Colleges are not mere schools. They are corporations
with a great deal of money invested in land, buildings and
equipment. The college administration is designed to provide
an orderly system in which instruction and learning can take
place.

Regents and Trustees. Some schools have a complex administrative structure (see the diagrams of university and
college structure on page 20).

If the university is public, its governing board or board
of directors is the Board of Regents. They are responsible to
the governor or the state legislature for the operation of the
school.

The members of the board are usually informed laymen
(rather than educators) from the fields of law, science and
industry. The school's charter states the manner in which
this board is chosen. In public institutions the board is either
elected by the people of the state or appointed by the governor or by some other state official or agency.

In private institutions the members of the board are
called "trustees." The board either chooses its own successors
(a self-perpetuating board) or, in denominational schools,
may be elected or appointed by the denomination.

Chancellor and President. Within the limits of the
school's charter and state laws, the board of regents or
board of trustees is responsible to manage the institution as
it sees fit. In practice, however, the board delegates most of
its executive function to an administrative officer it selects —
namely, the president. In a "multiuniversity" setting the top
officer may be the chancellor, who directs the presidents of a
number of universities under his jurisdiction.

In the United States a chancellor or president has a great deal of freedom to exercise his executive power and initiative. His tenure is not limited. That is, a president is not limited in the number of terms he may serve as president. I'll have more to say about "tenure" when I discuss faculty. **Vice-President, Provost and Deans.** The president is assisted by one or more vice-presidents and a number of administrative assistants. In large universities all educational activities are delegated to a provost or academic vice-president. In smaller institutions this function is filled by the academic dean. The provost or dean is responsible to the president for the selection of faculty members, organization of the curriculum, the quality of instruction and the academic budget. Complaints about the quality of education or of faculty members should be addressed to this person.

The Dean of Students. This person usually functions under the vice-president for student affairs. He maintains an office and staff to see that the student is taken care of in school and to help him solve problems relating to school. If this office doesn't handle the specific problem, someone there will be able to tell you who can help you.

Registrar. The registrar's office is responsible for academic records. It functions under the direction of the academic dean or dean of the college. If you have questions about your grades or if any are recorded incorrectly, this office will help you. The registrar's office handles transfer of credits from other schools and will also send your transcript (an official copy of your records) should you need it to go on to another school.

Other Important Administrative Officers. Students should know who the other important administrative officers are and what their function is. The *director of admissions* determines the eligibility of those who wish to be admitted as students. The *business officer* is responsible for the financial management of the school.

The Faculty. The faculty are not administrators, but they are part of the administrative structure of the school. You should be aware that there are various "ranks" of faculty

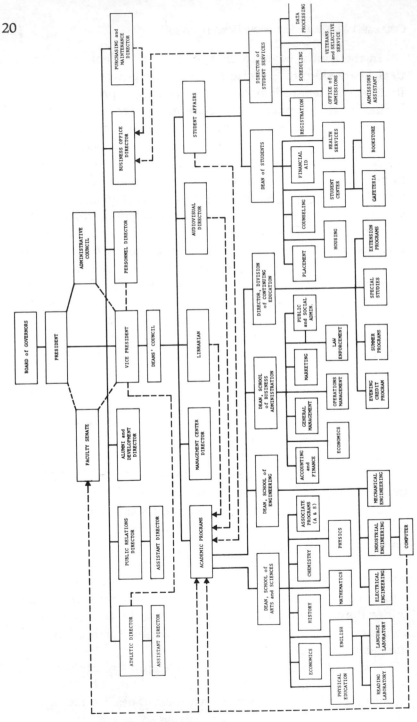

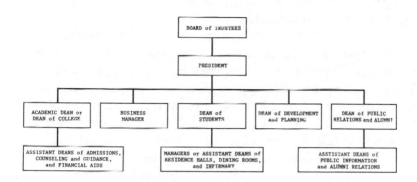

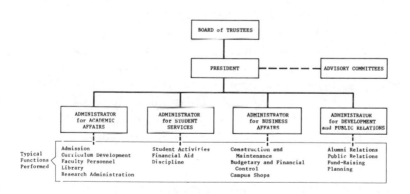

members. They are *professor, associate professor, assistant professor* and *instructor*. The Ph.D. is usually required for the professor and associate professor and the master's degree is normally the minimum requirement for appointment as assistant professor or instructor.

After stated periods of service, evidence of scholarly growth and teaching effectiveness, faculty members may be promoted. Those who qualify may be granted *tenure status*. Tenure means that they can be dismissed only for adequate cause, and formal procedure is usually required to terminate a tenured professor. Those without tenure are under yearly contract, which may or may not be renewed, depending on the institution's desire to retain the teacher.

It is important for a student to know this. A teacher *is* concerned with his or her effectiveness. It is a bread-and-butter matter, if nothing else. Properly registered complaints from the student body can help remedy classroom problems.

Schools and Departments. The university has a more complex organization than the college. It is made up of a number of degree-granting schools and colleges both at the undergraduate and graduate level, all under one administrative system.

The core is its liberal arts college. It also has a graduate school (stressing academic activity) and professional schools (stressing application of theory). The chart on page 20 lists the School of Engineering and the School of Business Administration as professional schools. The undergraduate, the entering freshman, is interested in the School (college) of Arts and Sciences and in the administrative staff of that college.

On page 21 you'll find an organizational chart of a typical college. It's more likely that the student of a college would have dealings with its president than a student in a university. But I have included the "upper echelon" officers on the chart so you will know how the school functions. The university student is more likely to have dealings with the deans, faculty and "lower echelon" administrative personnel.

IMPORTANT ADDITIONAL SERVICES
TO THE STUDENT

Student Advisors. These people may work out of the dean of students' office, but not necessarily. They are available to help you with information on class schedules, courses required for certain majors and your eligibility for different programs. Their job is to give you *academic counseling.* Personal counseling needs are referred to the counseling center or health unit.

Counseling Center/Career Counseling. These functions may be handled together or separately. Psychologists and/or counselors are available to help the student deal with personal problems that may be impairing his effectiveness. Christian students will want to be sure that they can feel comfortable with the counselor's perspective on Christianity because some counselors consider Christianity a neurosis, or the student's main problem. Your campus Christian fellowship or local church should be of help to you in finding a competent counselor who understands your Christian perspective.

Library. You will spend a lot of time here, so get acquainted with its layout, services and personnel. You will want to consider finding a regular place to study — where it's quiet and you're not distracted.

All of the material in the library is not in the stacks. Some is on microfilm and tape. Ask the librarian how to use this information and equipment and about any other services available.

Bookstore. Take time to go through the bookstore and see where everything is located. As soon as you register for your courses it is wise to get your books before they are sold out. Often, second-hand books are available. These can be a good buy. But be sure that you are buying the same edition the instructor is using in class. You may be able to buy the second edition second-hand, but it won't do you any good if your instructor is using the third edition in class.

Health Service. Remember that mom and dad aren't

around to take care of you, and it is your responsibility to find out what kind of health service is available for emergency care. Perhaps you can be treated on campus for minor problems. Major emergency care may have to be sought off-campus. Your dean of students office will know about this.

These are only some of the services available. For a comprehensive list of key people and services with whom you will want to become acquainted, Tim Walter's and Al Siebert's book *Student Success* is worth purchasing for its excellent appendix.[7]

CHRISTIAN ORGANIZATIONS

Many secular colleges accommodate Christian organizations as part of the university life. Often, schools provide rooms for campus ministries on their campus. Or, you may find them conveniently located adjacent to your campus. Some of the more familiar to evangelical Christians are Campus Crusade for Christ, Inter-Varsity Christian Fellowship and The Navigators. You also will want to check out the evangelical churches near the college. They can offer additional information about services available to the Christian student on campus.

At this point I want to raise a caution about a balance of involvement in Christian activities on campus. Some students go to the extreme of complete withdrawal from Christian activity, using the rationale that the primary reason for their being at school is to study. This is true enough, but a rounded college education involves more than study. Christian involvement in the world in which we live and the daily application of the knowledge we receive is essential to growth.

On the other hand, some students go to the extreme of becoming so involved in Bible study and witness that their education suffers. Unless you are paying your own way for your education, you have a responsibility to those who are helping you financially.

REVIEW QUESTIONS FOR CHAPTER 2

1. What is the difference between a junior college and a four-year college?

2. What is a "transfer program" in a junior college?

3. What is the difference between a college and a university?

4. Can a student go right from high school to seminary or other professional schools?

5. Is a four-year full-time program the only way you can get a college education?

6. What is the difference between "undergraduate" and "graduate" schools?

7. Match the proper letters and numbers of the two lists below. For example, the title (1) Regents or Trustees goes with the function (E) College Governing Board.

(1) Regents or Trustees

(2) Chancellor or President

(3) Provost or Dean

(4) Registrar

(5) Dean of Students

(6) Business Officer

(7) Tenure

(8) Student Advisor

(9) Counseling Center

(A) Financial manager of the school.

(B) An academic vice-president

(C) Responsible for the well-being of the students.

(D) With this, faculty can be dismissed only for adequate cause.

(E) College Governing Board

(F) Helps students deal with personal problems and plan careers.

(G) In charge of official student records.

(H) The chief administrative officer.

(I) Helps students with class schedules and required courses.

KEY

(F) (9)
(I) (8)
(D) (7)
(A) (6)
(C) (5)
(G) (4)
(B) (3)
(H) (2)
(E) (1)

CHAPTER THREE
Choosing A College

Though many people attend college with the idea that it will improve their economic opportunities, this should not be your sole aim. If it is, you may be disappointed. You may find that vocational education may be more to your liking.

The primary purpose of college is not to teach skills related to a job. Its purpose is to teach you to think and to learn. It goes beyond high school in helping you to develop your verbal and mathematical skills, which enables you to get a better grasp on the greatness of God's creation and live successfully in it. At the risk of oversimplification, I'll say that college is designed to help you think clearly and precisely. This ability should enable you to master effectively whatever job skills you eventually may need.

This is why you should not be concerned if you don't know what kind of job, career or vocation you are interested in. Theoretically, the first two years of college are to help you assess your interests and opportunities.

Be careful that you are not talked into going to college or that you do not attempt to talk someone into going when he's really not interested. College is not for everyone. I have four sons, each of whom made his own decision about college for different reasons.

Steve, my oldest, attended California State University at Fullerton. A strong motivation was an athletic scholarship and an opportunity to play college football. He felt at the time that this was a good way to get into professional football. He graduated with a major in physical education but instead of going into pro ball, Steve uses his skill as an exercise physiologist to manage a health club in Riverside, California.

Dave, my second son, put two years in the army. After two years in college on the G.I. Bill, he decided he wanted to learn a trade and work with his hands. He took an apprentice program at Todd Shipyard in Seattle and is now a journeyman pipefitter and welder.

Pete, my third son, finished high school in 1980. He couldn't stand the thought of more liberal arts education. Like his brother, Pete was interested in learning a trade and working with his hands. Dissatisfied with what the local vocational technical schools offered, he joined the navy under its guaranteed technical education program. He went through all the welding schools they offered and was certified to work on nuclear systems. After only two years, he enjoys the pay and benefits of a second class petty officer, a nice apartment in Pearl Harbor and interesting work on nuclear submarines.

Jonathan, my fourth son, is a senior in high school and is determined to win an athletic scholarship. He's interested in professional baseball and sees college ball as the way to go, with an education for his later years when he can no longer play ball. Associating with his baseball buddy, Mark, who is a good student, has also made him appreciate the value of an education.

WHY PEOPLE ATTEND COLLEGE

College is not for everyone. Nor is college essential for happiness and success in life. I expect that Dave and Pete will continue to be happy and successful in life because they are bright, ambitious and like their work. What is more, the motives for college are not always its scholastic value. People attend college for a variety of reasons. A recent study reveals at least seven:[1]

1. *Job Preparation.* Improving one's economic opportunities is the reason most students and parents suggest.

They see college as a means of providing either preparation
for a job, a credential needed to get a job, or a certification
of capability to hold a job.[2]

2. *Social Pressure.* One Colgate student claimed that he
was there because it was the only college he could get into
that his parents would not be ashamed to mention when
asked where he was attending school. A young woman,
though successful in her career, felt the need for a bachelor's
degree because her father, mother, brothers, aunts and
uncles all had at least bachelor's degrees and three held
doctorates.[3]

3. *Symbol of Upward Mobility.* Akin to social pressure is
the symbol of upward mobility. Some students are made to
feel that they don't belong to "the upper crust" if they don't
go to college. Even though this is not a good motive for college, the desire for upward mobility sometimes produces a
good student and a useful member of the work force.

4. *Maturity.* Just as some people enter military service as
a way to break from home and become mature away from
the influence of parents, some people go to college for the
same reason. Learning to make friends on your own and getting along with them while guarding your own values is an
important element in maturity. Though it may be an expensive way to grow up on your own, study after study has
shown that relationships and interaction with peers in college
is a most potent force for change in students.[4]

There is a major factor that the college-bound Christian
ought to consider when selecting a school. The moral climate
of various secular schools can differ sharply from what you
may have experienced at home and at high school. Consider
the reaction one person described to me:

"When I came to the university, I just wasn't prepared for
what I saw. I was a zombie for days. It just wouldn't sink
into my head that this was really going on here. But then I
realized that I can't ignore it. If this is what's going on, it's
even more reason to be out there teaching kids to handle it."

This was Phares Wood's reaction to the moral climate she
witnessed at an east coast university when she arrived there

in 1979. A graduate of Auburn University in Alabama, Phares had worked on Campus Crusade staff at the University of Alabama before coming east. She is neither immature nor naive. Phares is single, 26 years old, and has "been around the block" a few times. She is Senior Woman Staffer with Campus Crusade at her university. So the culture shock she underwent after her arrival had little to do with inexperience.

Phares believes that most secular schools in the Southeast are more conservative than elsewhere. At Auburn and the University of Alabama, stricter student regulations tend to control the open sexual promiscuity and drinking she discovered on the east coast university campus. "This university is a party school," says Phares.

Because not all secular colleges and universities are alike, Christian students may feel a lot more pressure to party and get involved sexually on some campuses than on others. This does not mean that those schools always ought to be out of the question for the Christian. Some Christians thrive in an atmosphere that challenges their faith. This was what I experienced when, as a new Christian, I joined the Air Force at age 17. My parents worried, but my time in the Air Force was the time of my greatest spiritual growth.

It is important, however, to assess how well you can handle blatant moral challenges to your faith. As Phares pointed out, the pressure at some schools is incredible. The administrations of some universities are very proud of their liberal points of view, which trickle down to their student body.

Therefore, the prospective student and parents should talk to Christian leaders on the campus of the school under consideration. They should also talk with other Christian students and try to assess the moral climate. Schools also publish their rules for students either in a separate rule book or in a larger publication such as the catalogue.

Because there are differences in the moral climate of various secular schools, it is most important that the Christian student be anchored firmly in a Christian fellowship

that will help him guard his values while he faces the rigors
of living with, working with and learning from non-
Christians.

5. *Intellectual Curiosity.* Both before entering and after
leaving college, students rank the desire to learn quite high.
If you're going to college you should want to learn. I don't
mean that students interested in vocations don't want to
learn. What I mean is that college is less concerned with
practical applications and vocational or technical training.

6. *Personal Problems.* Students often seek — or are shipped off to — schools that may offer them a new environment
in which they can solve personal problems. This is often true
of students entering Bible school or Christian college. These
are seen as "safe" places to overcome timidity and strengthen
weak spiritual convictions. Sometimes rebels are shipped off
to Christian schools with the idea that they'll get their act
together there.

It's less likely that the Christian student will go to a
secular college to solve personal problems. One problem that
Christian families attempt to solve is not so much with the
student as with the family. Sending the child to college is a
socially acceptable way to bring about a break in the parent-
child relation. This may be an acceptable, though expensive
way, to solve parent-child tensions. In a case like this the
family needs to be careful that it doesn't generate a whole
new set of problems that rise out of unrealistic
expectations — the parent for the child and the child for the
parent.

7. *Ulterior Motives.* During the 60s and '70s, one ulterior
motive in attending college was to avoid the draft.
Sometimes today the motive is to cash in on veterans'
benefits, grants or scholarships. Sometimes it's just to get
away from home or to postpone having to get a job. These
motives rarely auger well for a successful college career,
although it does happen. Parents often waste a great deal of
money, however, when the student is just trying to avoid
getting a full time job. This is why I suggest that a student

be expected to carry some of the expenses for his education. He is not so likely to waste his own money.

FACTORS AFFECTING CHOICE

Most students select a college with four factors in mind: geographic location, cost, program and ability to gain admission. Recent studies reveal that several other factors also influence a student's decision.[5]

Geographic Location. The closer the institution to home, the more likely the student will select it. Affluent students often travel greater distances because travel and new experiences tend to be part of their lifestyle already. But as a rule, most students will stay close to home, unless the geographical location has an unfavorable image. An inner city institution in a high crime area, for example, may not have the appeal of a country campus a little farther away.

Accessability to home is an important factor when it comes to weekends and holidays. I don't advise students to return home every weekend, but it is nice to be able to return on Thanksgiving, Christmas, Easter, and quarter or semester break.

Cost. Tuition and fees are important. Students are inclined to select less expensive schools. The annual outlay rather than the total expense for a full degree seems to be the usual rule of thumb in considering cost. Even though the school's academic year may permit you to complete a degree in three years rather than four, the asking price of the academic year can be a put-off.

You should not suppose, however, that the more expensive the school the higher the educational quality. It is entirely possible to pay big bucks for a blue chip school with famous professors and then to find that the professors are involved with research and are leaving the teaching to graduate assistants.

Convenience. Does the curriculum and academic term (quarter or semester) facilitate your work and family responsibilities? Most students must work to subsidize their education. Does the program facilitate this? Another important factor to consider is whether or not the program allows you to transfer credits from other schools. This is very important if you are considering community college. Find out ahead of time *if and where* you can transfer credits.

Traditional Relationships. Is this the "in" school to go to as far as your family or church is concerned? You may have to make a strong case for going against tradition, particularly if you expect the support of your family or church.

Institutional Reputation and Image. The institution of your choice should have the reputation of producing the kind of leader you aspire to be — whether athletic or religious. Whatever school won this year's Rose Bowl or produced the Heisman Trophy winner will be in great demand by aspiring football players. Which school has the image of producing top lawyers or physicians — or leaders in your field of interest?

Presence of Desired Program. If you do have a career goal in mind, be sure you select the school that will facilitate that goal. For example, if you are interested in a career in law, be sure to attend a college that provides the courses that adequately prepare you for pre-law and may even have a good image and rapport with professional schools of law. The same applies to pre-medical and medical college education.

Persuasion. To some degree persuasion plays a part in the selection of a college. It may be either direct or indirect. I mean that a coach, teacher, parent or pastor may be sold on a particular college. He may try to convince you that you should go. Or it may be their example as intelligent Christians that influences you. What worked for them may work for you — or it might not. You may respond differently to the school because you are a different person. Every school has a personality. Does it fit *your* personality?

Whim or Accident. The Christian who thinks in terms of God's sovereignty does not think in terms of whims or accidents. I use these words to describe the human side of the decision. Sometimes a last-minute decision in August will prompt a student to go where his friends are going. Sometimes an unexpected opportunity may present itself. Don't ignore unexpected open doors merely because they are not part of your plan. By the same token, just because the opportunity is there, that doesn't mean it is right for *you*.

COLLEGES THAT ATTRACT

Students tend to gravitate toward colleges that meet their needs. In choosing a college it is well to consider what kind of colleges attract students and compare them to your college.

The Carnegie Foundation for the Advancement of Teaching has found that schools attracting large numbers of students have the following characteristics:

1. They attract all ages rather than just the ideal college student in the 18- to 21-year bracket.

2. They provide for part-time as well as full-time students.

3. They are less, rather than more, dependent on teacher education as part of their curriculum.

4. They have public state support.

5. They are large enough to accomplish their objectives.

6. They are in an urban rather than a rural location.

7. They have comparatively low tuition and few local competitors.

8. They either have a national reputation or a devoted specialized constituency.

9. They are older institutions.

10. They made wise commitments in the '60s, when other schools became over-committed.

11. They have a stabilized undergraduate enrollment rather than a volitale graduate enrollment.

12. They are related to health professions.

13. They are in sound financial condition.

14. They are closely related to reality.

15. They are in the South, California or New York rather

than in other parts of the country, particularly the North
Plains and Mountain States.[6]

During the '50s and '60s these institutions competed for
the ideal college students who were between the ages of 18
and 22, whose combined SAT scores were 1100 and above,
who maintained a high school average of B+ or better, and
who were economically comfortable.

In the '80s and '90s this is changing. The number of such
18-year-olds will decline by one-fourth (one million),
whereas the number of schools will increase by one-third.
The competition for students will be fierce, which is to the
advantage of the student who should never forget that he is
a *consumer* of education. He will be in a "buyer's market."
Even less able students will benefit. For schools to survive
financially, they must make room for students they might
not have accepted in earlier years.

WHO GOES WHERE TO COLLEGE?

In the previous discussion we looked at colleges that attract. After all, students must have a good reason for going
to these colleges.

Let's look at it from another angle. Let's look at the student and consider who goes where to college. Alexander
Astin, Director of Research for the American Council of
Education, gathered information from over 127,000 freshmen
in 248 colleges and universities to determine why they chose
the college they did. He came up with six factors that influenced their decision to attend the schools they chose. He
calls them "Freshmen Input Factors":

1. Intellectualism
   a. High academic aptitude (especially mathematical
      aptitude)
   b. High percentage of students who intend to obtain
      graduate degrees (especially the Ph.D.)
   c. High percentage of students who intend to become
      scientists
   d. High percentage of Merit Scholars
   e. High average grades in high school

      f.   High percentage of students who have won awards·in science contests
2. Estheticism
      a. High percentage of students who have exhibited works of art and have won art awards
      b. High percentage of students planning careers in artistic fields (art, music, writing, etc.)
      c. High percentage of students who have won literary awards
      d. High percentage of students who have published poems or articles
      e. High percentage of students who edited high school publications
      f.   High percentage of girls in the student body
3. Status
      a. High percentage of students planning enterprising careers (lawyers, business executives, politicians, etc.)
      b. High average socioeconomic level of students' fathers
      c. High percentage of students undecided about career choice and field of study
      d. High percentage of students planning to obtain professional degrees
4. Leadership
      a. High percentage of students who were elected to student offices in high school
      b. High percentage of students who had leads in high school or church plays
      c. High percentage of students who won awards in speech or debate contests in high school
5. Pragmatism
      a. High percentage of students planning realistic types of careers (for example, engineer, farmer, forest ranger)
      b. Low percentage of students planning social types of careers (for example, schoolteacher, nurse, social worker)
6. Masculinity
      a. High percentage of male students
      b. Low percentage of students planning social types of careers
      c. High percentage of students planning to obtain professional degrees
      d. Low percentage of students who won awards in musical competition in high school[7]

The study further revealed that the type of school the student chose reflected the importance he placed on each factor:

Freshman Input Factor	Types of Institutions with the Highest Scores	Types of Institutions with the Lowest Scores
Intellectualism	Technological institutions Private nonsectarian liberal arts colleges	Public liberal arts colleges Teachers colleges Protestant liberal arts colleges
	Private nonsectarian universities	
Estheticism	Private nonsectarian liberal arts colleges	Catholic universities
	Catholic liberal arts colleges	
Status	Private nonsectarian liberal arts colleges	Teachers colleges Public liberal arts colleges Technological institutions
	Protestant universities Private nonsectarian universities	
Leadership	Private nonsectarian liberal arts colleges	Technological institutions Catholic liberal arts colleges
Pragmatism	Technological institutions	Catholic liberal arts colleges Teachers colleges Private nonsectarian liberal arts colleges
	Public universities	
Masculinity	Catholic universities	Catholic liberal arts colleges Teachers colleges[8]
	Private nonsectarian universities	

HOW TO CHOOSE YOUR COLLEGE

If by now your mind is boggled and you don't have the faintest idea of how to choose your college, take hope. Remember that most students use the simple formula: geographical location, cost, program, and ability to gain admission. The rest of the information I have given you is to help you refine this simple formula.[9]

You will also want to look at the appendix in this book, "Study In U.S. Colleges and Universities." It is a selected bibliography of books that provide practical information on programs, fields of study, degrees, costs and other topics relevant to study in U.S. colleges.

The bibliography is divided into three parts: general directories and guides; directories and other reference works in specific fields (everything from anthropology to sociology); and general information. It is not necessary to buy any of these references. You should be able to find them through your library system. If you are a pastor or student advisor, you may want to get several of the more helpful ones to use with those whom you advise.

Let me make two more suggestions that may help you implement this information. Find out what your interests are by taking some interest inventories and make a checklist when you start considering what college you want to go to.

Interest Inventory. I have made it clear that college is not designed to prepare you for a specific vocation. You may find it helpful, however, to take some psychological testing to determine your area of interest.

In 1947, when I was 16 years old, I took a battery of tests at the Johnson-O'Connor Human Engineering Laboratory in New York City to determine what vocation would most likely bring me success. The results suggested that I would do well as a minister, teacher and writer. At age 51 I look back on a successful career involving all three.

This kind of testing is immensely valuable. I recommend three tests, though it may not be necessary to take all three. The first is the "Myers-Briggs Type Indicator." This test focuses on the "type" of person you are. The types are broken down into four groups and 16 sub-groups. Are you a sensing-intuitive type? Are you an introvert or extrovert? Various "types" tend to gravitate toward certain careers.

The second is the Strong-Campbell Interest Inventory. It assesses your interest in occupations, school subjects, activities, amusements, types of people, preference of activities and your characteristics. This test reveals what careers would most likely offer you success. The third is the Jackson Vocational Interest Survey (JVIS). This survey assesses work roles and work styles.

Psychologists and some other therapists are equipped to do this testing. If you cannot find someone in your area, write me in care of:

Here's Life Publishers, Inc.
P.O. Box 1576
San Bernardino, CA 92402

You may also reach me by phone at (301) 464-0985.

Checklist. After you determine your "type" and area of interest, use a checklist to sort out your choice of college. Here are fifteen of the most frequently considered issues and questions asked. Write the names of the colleges you are considering in the appropriate spaces, and then rate them according to the scale suggested from a 1 (poor) to a 5 (superior). Apply a numerical value to each question. You will want to consider applying to the institution that comes up with the highest numerical total. This is only a suggestion, however. Some of the issues may be more important than others and should be weighted with more importance.

Scale   Colleges

1 = Poor
2 = Below average
3 = Average
4 = Above average
5 = Superior

- Type of training offered. Does this school offer the program(s) I want?   _____
- Accreditation and national reputation. If I go to this school will it mean anything to the educationally aware?   _____
- Faculty. Does this school have the kind of faculty that can meet my needs?   _____
- Location. Is the school's geographical location convenient?   _____
- Size and type of college. Is this college too big or too small for me?   _____
- Admission requirements. Can I get into this college?   _____

- Housing. Is the housing adequate (live at home, in private dwelling off campus, dormitory)?   _____
- Faculty availability. Can I make contact with this faculty or is it overloaded or removed to research?   _____
- Cost and financing. Can I afford this school and finance my education here?   _____
- Transferring. Will this school accept transfer credits from a community college or my four-year college?   _____
- Personality. Do I fit on this campus?   _____
- Degree. Will a degree from this school assist me in achieving my future goals?   _____
- Student body. Is the nature of the student body consistent with my own intellectual capability and diverse enough to stimulate my personal growth?   _____
- Intellectual excitement. Is there a tradition of academic innovation and intellectual excitement?   _____
- Program and personal need. Will the programs on campus meet my personal needs, not just the academic?   _____

Every institution has a personality. Try to match yours to the institution and you will find that your choice most likely will be a good one.

REVIEW FOR CHAPTER 3

1. Is the moral climate at all secular schools the same?
2. True or false: People attend college for a variety of reasons.
3. True or false: The four most common reasons students choose a college are geographic location, cost, program and ability to gain admission.
4. Discuss this statement: The purpose of college is to teach you job skills.
5. Why do you want to attend the college of your choice?
6. What kind of a job or career would you like to have when you graduate from college?

Answers to questions 1 — 3:
1. No 2. True 3. True

CHAPTER FOUR
Financing Your Education

"If my daughter can plow through all of this information successfully, get financial aid and get into college, she doesn't need a college education." This was the sentiment of a mother who was trying to help her daughter find her way through the maze of financial programs and admissions procedures. The process is indeed overwhelming at times, but I've tried to simplify it in this chapter by taking it step by step.

FINDING THE MONEY

The financial aid office at every college has information on available assistance programs. They also have the forms you will need to apply for aid. You should know, however, what kind of aid is generally available so you may be able to talk intelligently about it with the aid officer. In fact, so many programs are available, your aid officer may not be able to keep track of all of them. Grants and loans as well as scholarships are available through the government and in the private sector.

Federal Financial Aid Programs. There are five basic federally funded assistance programs, for which dollar amounts are determined yearly.[1] The first of these programs is the basic *Pell Grant Program* (formerly called the Basic Grant Program). If the school is an approved institution, and if you are an undergraduate enrolled on at least a half-time basis, you may be eligible for a grant, which means you don't have to pay it back. The grants are usually small. In 1982-83 award period (July 1, 1982-June 30, 1983) they will range from $50 to $1,674. Application forms are available from your college financial aid office, high schools, and public libraries.

Another federal program is the *Supplemental Educational Opportunity Grant* (SEOG) *Program.* This is for students who must drop out if they cannot get emergency financial aid. You are eligible to apply if you are enrolled at least half-time as an undergraduate or vocational student in an educational institution participating in the program. Graduate students are not eligible. This grant is made on the basis of need and available funds. Currently, if you receive an SEOG, it cannot be less than $200 or more than $2,000 a year. To apply, contact the financial aid office at your college.

The third program is the *National Direct Student Loan Program* (NDSL). The school of your choice may have government-supported money for low-cost student loans. At this writing, you can get $2,500 for the first two years of college or for a vocational program; $5,000 total for all undergraduate years; $10,000 for graduate school. You don't start paying on the loan until nine months after graduation. You have ten years to pay at 3 percent interest. If you go into some needed career fields, your loan may be reduced or forgiven.

The fourth federal aid program is the *Guaranteed Student Loan Program* (GSL). Under GLS a financial institution such as a bank makes the loan, which is guaranteed by a federally designated state agency. Currently, you can borrow up to $2,500 for each undergraduate year and the interest cannot exceed seven percent. For all your undergraduate years the loan cannot exceed $7,500. In many cases the federal government will pay the interest on the loan while the student is in school. Your state maintains an office that will give you the information you need, or you can ask your financial aid office.

Finally, there is the *College Work-Study Program* (CWSP or CW-S). Under this program the government picks up most of the cost for your work on campus—up to fifteen hours a week. The school's financial aid office decides who is eligible for the program and hands out the jobs. Remember that all of these programs change yearly. **Other Kinds of Programs.** *College Knowledge,*[2] the book I've mentioned before, lists other programs: Catalogue of Federal Assistance Programs, 1980. This catalogue replaces the old "Green Book," technically known as "Federal and State Student Aid Programs, 1972." The subtitle of the catalogue of federal assistance programs is, "An Indexed Guide To the Federal Government's Programs Offering Educational Benefits To the American People." It's a Department of Education book. The code number is 065-000-00031-8 and can be purchased for $9.50. Write to:

The Superintendent of Documents
U.S. Government Printing Office
Washington, D.C. 20402

The Harry S. Truman Scholarship Foundation. This foundation offers scholarships to juniors who have a potential for public service. For information write:

Harry S. Truman Scholarship Foundation
712 Jackson Place, N.W.
Washington, D.C. 20006

State Programs. For information on state administered scholarships and grants write the National Association of State Scholarship and Grant Programs:

NASSGP Annual Survey
c/o ISSC
102 Wilmot Rd.
Deerfield, IL 60615

Aid for Women. Send for the pamphlet, "Educational Financial Aid Sources for Women."

c/o Administrator
Clairol Loving Care Scholarship Program
345 Park Ave—5th Floor
New York, NY 10022

Help for Journalists. Send for "The Journalism Scholarship Guide."

The Newspaper Fund
P.O. Box 300
Princeton, NJ 08540

Aid for the Arts. This expensive guide ($13.95 in paperback) is called "The National Directory of Grants and Aid To Individuals in the Arts." Perhaps your library can get a copy. It is available from:

WIAL
Box 9005
Washington, D.C. 20003

Rhodes and Fulbright Scholarships. You must be very bright to be awarded either of these. Rhodes is for juniors and Fulbright is for students who have received their bachelor's degree. Write:

The Rhodes Scholarship Office
Wesleyan University
Middletown, CT 06457

Additional Sources. Get "The Ambitious Students Guide To Scholarships and Loans" ($1.50). It offers 150 sources you probably won't find anywhere else. Write:

Octameron Associates
Box 3437
Alexandria, VA 22302

Your college catalogues may also list scholarships and grants available through the school. The financial aid office at the college can help you determine your eligibility for their programs.

If you haven't found a grant or scholarship yet, don't give up. There's got to be one for you! Perhaps if you hammer tacks with your left hand in a furniture factory on Thursdays, you may qualify. Although this may sound a bit facetious, the fact is there are a multitude of sources of aid. There truly seems to be something for everyone. For less than a dollar you can get "A Guide to Student Assistance." Write the U.S. Government Printing Office, Washington, D.C. 20402. The booklet details where you can find financial assistance in the fields of library science, foreign language, science, nursing, public health, vocational rehabilitation, teaching, education of the handicapped, and water pollution control. In addition they list the G.I. Bill, military academies, war orphan education, ROTC, Coast Guard, Merit Scholarships, National Honor Society Scholarships, union scholarships and awards, scholarships for Indians and Blacks, General Motors and Alfred P. Sloan Scholarships.

When all else fails, turn to *Need a Lift?*[3] I believe it is the number one scholarship and career handbook on the market today. To get your copy, phone your local American Legion Post, or write to

The American Legion
National Emblem Sales
P.O. Box 1055
Indianapolis, IN 46206

Talk about a treasure trove, this 137-page paperback is packed with valuable information, and its copious indexes help you find the information you want! The cost is one dollar, post paid!

Need A Lift? Offers specific details including undergraduate sources of financial assistance, and where and how to apply. Let me whet your appetite by listing some of these sources of scholarships and aid:

Extension of Social Security Benefits To Students Attending School After Reaching Age 18 and Up To Age 22.

Army, Navy and Air Force ROTC

The U.S. Coast Guard Academy

The U.S. Merchant Marine Academy

The New Mexico Military Institute

The Railroad Retirement Act

Bell & Howell Schools Scholarship Program

The American College for the Applied Arts

Education for the Handicapped, Public Law 91-230

National Achievement Scholarship Program for Outstanding negro Students

The Elks Foundation Scholarship Awards

National 4-H Council

The American Society for Metals Foundation for Education and Research

The National Association of Secondary School Principals and the National Honor Society

The Association of Independent Colleges and Schools

Science Talent Search

Entomological Society of America

AMOCO Foundation, Inc.

The College of Insurance

The Shell Companies Foundation, Inc.

This information-packed booklet lists 21 more sources of scholarships or financial aid for undergraduates only, and 24 more for both graduate and undergraduate students. There must be something for you here!

GETTING ORGANIZED

Although the task seems insurmountable, organizing your correspondence and inquiries about financial aid will be valuable to you later. First, make a correspondence chart to help you keep track of your correspondence on financial aid. It should include the name and address of the organization, type of aid (loan, grant, scholarship), date written, date of reply and what you have done about it. Just take a sheet of notebook paper and set it up this way:

Letter Written To:	Type of aid (L) (G) (Sc)	Date Written	Date of Reply	What I've Done About It

Next, purchase a simple accordion-type file from your office supply store. It should have several compartments in it. Keep your correspondence chart in it, together with copies of your letters and the replies. A small appointment calendar would be helpful, too. Having everything together in one place will help eliminate confusion. As your material accumulates, you might want to purchase a file folder for each of the organizations you are dealing with and keep them in a regular file box.

At this point I need to tell you about the College Board. It is a nonprofit membership organization that provides tests and other educational services for students, schools and colleges. The membership is composed of more than 2,500 colleges, school systems and education associations. Representatives of the members serve on the Board of Trustees and advisory councils and committees that consider the programs of the College Board and participate in determining its policies and activities.

Because institutions vary in the amount and type of aid they offer, you will want to chart your comparisons of the aid available at several different schools. You may discover scholarships are available to you at one school but not at another. The College Board puts out an excellent guide for adult students, *Paying for Your Education,*[4] which offers the following comparison guide to help you collect and compare information on the various colleges. This guide gives you an idea of the right questions to ask when you are weighing the differences. You may need to make additional copies of the guide if you are considering more than two institutions.

COMPARISON GUIDE

	Institution 1	Institution 2
Names of the institutions you are considering...............	_____	_____
Name of the financial aid officer	_____	_____
Office hours...................	_____	_____
Telephone number...........	_____	_____

Aid Programs:
Is the institution eligible to
award federal and state student
aid?.......................... _____   _____
Does it participate in all federal
and state programs?........... _____   _____
Does it offer any aid programs
of its own?................... _____   _____
Would you qualify?........... _____   _____

Policies and Practices:
What formal or informal prac-
tices are used to award aid?.... _____   _____
What types of students receive
first preference?.............. _____   _____
Does the institution have a
deferred tuition policy?........ _____   _____
Does it offer advanced standing? _____   _____

Forms and Deadlines:
What is the admissions deadline,
if any?....................... _____   _____
Is there a preferred deadline?... _____   _____
What financial forms are
required?..................... _____   _____
                               _____   _____
                               _____   _____
What form should be used for
the Pell Grant?.............. _____   _____
Where should you send the
completed application?......... _____   _____

Cost:
How much does the institution
indicate your total budget to be?
It should cover tuition and fees,
books and supplies, living costs,
personal expenses,
transportation................ _____   _____

Aid Awards:
When you have been offered
financial aid, you can compare
how much it will cost to attend
the institutions to which you
have applied. Probably each
financial aid offer will differ, as
will the costs of attending each
school. Consider:
Total expense budget.......... _____   _____

Minus expected student
contribution................. _____   _____
Equals net needed to attend the
institution................... _____   _____
Minus grant aid offered by the
institution................... _____   _____
Minus load offered........... _____   _____
Minus work-study offered...... _____   _____
Equals unmet need........... _____   _____

The College Board suggests that you compare the total cost of the institutions you are interested in attending. Are you willing to pay more for one college than another? Considering other aid income, which schools will you be best able to afford? Remember, if the college you select cannot meet your financial need, you will have to cover this amount yourself either by cutting your costs, or through special aid programs, or with an educational loan.

You will therefore need to develop a *financial aid worksheet*. The worksheet below[5] is adapted from *Paying for Your Education*.

You will see from the worksheet that deadlines for financial aid applications are very important and sometimes very strict. Each college has its own deadlines for financial applications and admission. Many have two financial aid deadlines: an early, "preferred" deadline that gives an applicant the best chance for getting aid; and a final deadline after which no applications are accepted. Ask about these deadlines early and record them in the proper place on your worksheet, on your family calendar, and on your little appointment calendar. Keep this worksheet in your file, too:

Steps to Take	When to Take Them
————Step 1————	
Take time to read over the financial aid material you have already gathered. If you have any questions, write them down so that you can ask your college financial aid officer.	Start right now. The earlier you start, the better are your chances of getting all the aid that is available to you.

————————Step   2————————

Send for any additional financial aid information you think might be helpful. If it seems to meet your needs, find out more about it, and apply.

As early as possible.

————————Step   3————————

Find out what state student aid programs are available in your state, how to apply, and who is eligible. Ask your aid officer, or contact your state higher education department.

As early as you can. Write down any deadlines on your aid calendar.

————————Step   4————————

Ask for free information on federal student aid programs. Get the "Five Federal Financial Aid Programs" booklet. Call 800-683-6700.

After January 1 of the year you wish to apply. Programs and program eligibility rules change, so check again around the time you plan to study.

————————Step   5————————

Prepare an estimate of your financial need. You will need to know how much you will be expected to pay before you can get aid. When you send in your financial aid application (Step 7), you will find out if you qualify for aid and, if so, how much. For help in preparing your estimate, send for *Meeting College Costs*, College Board Publication Orders, Box 2815, Princeton, NJ 08541. It's free.

After January 1 of the year you wish to apply.

————————Step   6————————

Call or write to the institutions where you would like to study, and ask for financial aid information. In addition to inquiring about aid programs, be sure to find out in each case what is used as an estimated student budget to establish aid. Study the information using the Comparison Guide on pages 47-49.

Five or six months before you would like to begin to study or before the academic term starts at the institution of your choice. If you are studying now, you should look into the possibility of financial aid to help continue your studies.

————————Step   7————————

Obtain the financial aid applications,

Any time after January 1 of the

especially for the Basic Pell Grant Program. If you think you will need help in completing these forms, see your college financial aid officer.

year you are applying for, but at least two months before the deadline at each institution you are considering. Mark these dates on your calendar.

──────Step 8──────

Plan a time when you are able to spend several hours on your applications. Make sure you have a pencil, pen and scratch paper; then sit down with a copy of your most recent federal income tax return and complete the applications.[6]

As soon as the applications arrive.

──────Step 9──────

Mail the applications. Be sure to apply for the Pell Grant. Do not apply for GSL or other loans at this point, because if you apply for and receive a loan before you apply for other aid, the amount of aid that you could receive from other sources might be reduced. Use certified mail, if possible.

As soon as you have completed Step 8.

──────Step 10──────

You should receive a Student Eligibility Report (SER) for the Pell Grant approximately four to six weeks after you mail your application. Mark this date on your calendar. If you do not receive the SER within that time call 800-638-6700 and ask about your application, or write to Pell Grants, P.O. Box T, Iowa City, IA 52240.

──────Step 11──────

Use your SER to search for aid.

──────Step 12──────

Send all three pages of the SER to each institution you would like to attend. If you are considering more than one institution, make photocopies of the SER, or call the 800 number listed above to request duplicates.

As soon as you receive your SER.

──────Step   13──────

Each financial aid office will send a rejection or acceptance notice.

Find out what month each institution will send out notices. Mark these dates on your calendar.

──────Step   14──────

Once you receive an award notice, make an assessment. Use the Comparison Guide (see pages 47-49) to compare offers. Look at the deadline date when you must accept or reject the offer, and mark it on your calendar.

As soon as possible after you receive the award notices, but before the deadline by which you must either accept or reject the award.

──────Step   15──────

Now is the time for a final decision. Weigh all factors, including cost. Accept one offer and reject all others — and respond to each institution by the deadline. Now is the time to consider a loan. You may have to check with several lenders in order to get a loan. Look into GSL.

At least 10 weeks before your semester or quarter begins.

Some Hints. Remember that eligibility rules and your financial circumstances change, so apply again next year, even if you did not get aid the first year you apply. Don't let yourself become discouraged. There are many forms and applications to fill out, but if you need money for your education, it will be well worth your time to apply.

Read everything through at least once and learn the ins and outs of the programs before starting to fill out applications. That will save a lot of time and avoid many complications. If you are still confused and have questions for which you can't find answers, see a college financial aid officer. Don't be afraid to ask questions. When you talk to someone, ask for and write down his name and title. Persist in your questions until you understand. Keep a record of everything you do. Work for your rightful benefits.

ALTERNATIVE WAYS TO EARN CREDIT TOWARD A DEGREE

What happens if you have explored all of these avenues

of financial assistance, and you have discovered that you are still unable to afford the traditional full-time, four-year day school program? Don't give up—there are alternatives that can offer you bonafide, quality credit at a blue chip college at a much lower cost than traditional programs require. Higher education in the United States is no longer limited to rigidly scheduled classroom courses attended by the economically elite.

You may find that you can put together a package with a four-year college whereby you can get some of your credits by correspondence and the rest through a combination of day school or extension school work on or off campus, and you may be able to carry a part or full-time job while you do it. I know of many married students and students from low-income families who have received an excellent education this way. There are five basic alternatives:

1. *Correspondence and Independent Study.* Seventy-three colleges and universities who are members of the National University Extension Association (NUEA) Division of Independent Study offer college credit through correspondence instruction. The courses are taught through the material they send to the student and are graded by the same standards used in classroom instruction.

A complete description of the courses offered and how to take the program can be found in the "NUEA Guide To Independent Study Through Correspondence Instruction." Send $2.00 to:

National University Extension Association
Suite 360
One DuPont Circle, N.W.
Washington, D.C. 20036

Generally, correspondence instruction is open to adults without regard to their educational background. However, some schools require prerequisites for certain courses.

Schools granting credit are not just obscure ones like Coyote College of Podunk Junction. The State University of New York, a nationally respected university, offers a biology course that covers enrollment, a home laboratory kit, a study guide and reading materials. At this writing it costs $53.55. Private correspondence schools also offer instruction. You will want to be sure that you exercise the same caution here that I suggest with a junior college program. If you intend to transfer your correspondence credit to a four-year college program later and continue your education in a traditional day school program, *be sure* the school you are interested in will accept the transfer credits. Generally, universities and colleges limit the amount and the kind of correspondence credit they will apply toward their degree.

One innovative program run by the University of California, San Diego (UCSD) Extension, offers courses by television, newspaper, radio and cassette. Schools subscribing to this program may determine how credit may be earned. UCSD supplies all the material.

2. *Credit By Examination.* Under this program it doesn't matter *how* you gained your knowledge of the subject. If you can demonstrate proficiency in it, you can get credit by an examination designed to measure your proficiency.

The most extensive program is the College Level Examination Program (CLEP) offered through the New York-based College Entrance Examination Board. This board does not grant credit, but it sends the scores of those who pass the exams to colleges and universities that do award credit for passing scores. More than 1,800 schools in the United States grant credit for the successful completion of these tests. In 1976 alone almost 100,000 people took the tests. These tests are not easy, but you have nothing to lose by trying.

CLEP exams are held the third week of each month at more than 900 test centers throughout the United States. If you live more than 150 miles away from a test center, special arrangements can be made for you.

Two types of CLEP are offered: general exams and subject exams. The general exams cover English composition, humanities, mathematics, natural science, and social science/history. The general tests last one hour and ask multiple choice questions. Exams covering 47 different subjects are offered. They are 90-minute multiple choice exams.

The fee for CLEP exams, paid in advance, is $20 for one, $30 for two taken at one sitting, and $40 for three to five taken at one sitting.

You can obtain more information about CLEP equivalency testing by writing:

CLEP
College Board, Dept. C
888 Seventh Ave.
New York, NY 10019

You should be aware that there are other equivalency exams.

If CLEP does not offer the subject matter you want, or if the degree course you are interested in requires a different kind of exam, you should then consider a national testing program called the Proficiency Examination Program (PEP), which is offered through the American College Testing Program (ACT). The exams, called ACT-PEP, are offered four times a year at various military bases and colleges. Fifty different tests are offered.

These exams are divided into two parts — the College Proficiency Examinations Program (CPEP) and the Regents External Degree Examinations (REDE). Fees range from $25 to $35 for a CPEP exam and from $25 to $150 for REDEs. Write for more information to:

ACT-PEP
P.O. Box 168
Iowa City, IA 52240

In New York write:

New York State Department of Education
Room 1919
99 Washington Ave.
Albany, NY 12230

3. *Credit for Noncollegiate Instruction.* It is possible that you have already been taking college-level courses without earning deserved college credit. About 13 million people take courses through their businesses, labor unions, government agencies and volunteer and professional organizations each

year, and much of the work can be credited toward a college degree.

The American Council on Education's (ACE) Office on Educational Credit (OEC) sponsors several programs designed to evaluate such courses and make recommendations to colleges about the amount of credit that should be granted. More than 6,000 courses offered by the Department of Defense alone have been granted credit in 1,700 colleges and universities.

Servicemen — particularly those in the army who are classified under the Military Occupations Speciality System — should investigate the possibility of gaining credit for skills learned in the service. The OEC's annual publication, "A Guide to the Evaluation of Educational Experiences in the Armed Services," tells what skills receive credit. You may be able to get a copy through your library. Otherwise, send $7.50 to:

American Council on Education
Publications Division
One DuPont Circle, N.W.
Washington, D.C. 20036

Another project by the OEC, run in cooperation with the New York State Board of Regents, has catalogued 1,000 courses run by 80 community organizations that offer college credit. These are listed in "A Guide To Educational Programs in Noncollegiate Organizations." If your library does not have it, send $6.00 to the Project of Noncollegiate-Sponsored Education at the ACE address given above.

4. *Credit for Experience.* Educators recognize that experience is a good teacher. A program called "Cooperative Assessment of Experimental Learning" (CAEL) is attempting to help people cash in on their experience. This program, run by the Educational Testing Service (ETS) and 200 cooperative schools, is being developed to sharpen methods for evaluating learning through experience.

For one to obtain credit under this program, learning must be documented, it must fit properly into a degree program, and credit should be based on a portfolio assembled by the student with the help of advisers. Evaluation through standardized tests such as CLEP or CPEP is most effective.

Both volunteer work and homemaking skills qualify, and your work at church such as youth group leader or treasurer has potential. Work categories that qualify are put together on "I Can" lists. Books publishing these lists can be obtained by writing:

Educational Testing Service
Princeton, NJ 08540

5. *Limited On- and Off-Campus Degree Programs.* On-campus programs for part-time students have been available for 50 years. Now off-campus programs are also available. The student attends class on campus for a limited time only—perhaps for one or two weeks. The time limit for completing a degree may be extended, and credit for learning gained through experience may also be granted. The off-campus part-time student must meet the same requirements that students meet for full-time on-campus study.

The on-campus degree program differs from the traditional degree program in that the courses are offered on campus in the evening, weekends and in the summer. Students have the full use of all the campus facilities. Columbia University in New York City has such a program. Though it is on campus, the cost is less than that of the regular full-time program. Here is a case where a quality education is available at a quality school, but at a reduced cost.

A variety of the off-campus program is the off-campus independent study degree program. The Empire State College of New York has such a program. Regional centers are located throughout New York State. With faculty advisors (called "mentors"), students make contracts describing what, how, and when the student will study. The cost is quite reasonable: $375 per sixteen weeks for state residents with less than 56 credits and $600 for out-of-state residents with fewer than 56 credits.

Finally, you may want to consider a RED degree—The New York Regent's External Degree. Anyone in the United

States can apply. This program is supervised by faculty and administrators from New York colleges and universities. It grants credit for college courses taken at other institutions, for proficiency exams (CLEP, ACT-PEP, CPEP, REDE), for courses sponsored by military educational programs, for knowledge or skills that cannot be readily evaluated by tests (known in some schools as Assessment of Prior Learning), and for courses offered by nonacademic organizations (see page 55).

There is no time limit for completing studies for a Regents External Degree. Charges include $75 for enrollment, $25 to $50 per year for record maintenance, and $25 graduation fee. Counselors are available to advise students, and the program is approved for veterans' education benefits.[7]

If you are having a tough time financing your education, you will want to consider seriously these alternatives to earning college credit towards a degree.

Alternative education may not have the snob appeal of a full-time day program at a well-known college, but a tailor-made program can offer a solid education with a respectable degree at a much lower cost — possibly at the same school.

ADMISSION

Whether you decide to use an alternative method of earning your degree or to pursue a more traditional approach, you will need to file applications for admission to the schools of your choice. First select the best financial aid program for you, and notify (in writing) the other programs of your decision. Then be certain to meet the deadlines for applications for admissions.

Colleges subscribing to the Candidates Reply Agreement (CRDA) will not require you to notify the college of your decision to attend (or to accept an offer of financial aid) before May 1 of the year you apply if you are an incoming freshman. The purpose of the agreement is to give all applicants time to hear from all the colleges to which they have applied before having to make a commitment to any one of them.

By the time you have selected your financial aid program, you should have obtained the application for admission forms from the colleges of your choice. As you did with the financial aid form, plan a time when you are able to spend at least an hour on each application. Be sure that you have your high school transcript, SAT scores, and any other documentation required for admission.

The admission form is to help the school determine whether or not you are qualified for admission. Find out when you can expect to get a response on your application. Some schools have rolling admissions, which means you can be admitted as soon as the school receives all documents showing that you are qualified.

REGISTRATION AND ORIENTATION

Once you have been accepted for admission, you must decide which school you will attend and notify the others of your decision. Remember that a letter of admission merely qualifies you to attend the school; it is not enough that you made application and have been accepted, before you can attend classes, you must be officially registered.

Upon admission to the college or university, you will receive information about orientation and registration. It is important that you attend the orientation program. It will help you become acquainted with the school, and it will help you register for your first semester. Some schools even offer an orientation for parents, too. See your catalogue for information, or call your Student Affairs Office.

Instructions on how to register are found in the schedule of classes, which will be issued to you at the beginning of the semester. If you have attended orientation, you should have a good idea of the when, where, and how of registration.

It is important, also, to remember that not all schools have a deferred payment plan. If your school does not, you will be expected to settle your account at registration time, or you cannot be registered.

Once you register, you will be officially enrolled. You will find out when and where each of your classes meets. Each course will have an official class list on which your name must appear for you to be allowed to attend class.

There will be a period of approximately 10 class days in which you may adjust your schedule. You may drop or add courses or change sections with no charge.

After this schedule adjustment period, all courses in which you are enrolled become a permanent part of your record. In most schools you will be considered a full-time student if you are enrolled for nine or more credit hours, though this may vary from school to school.

For several weeks after the schedule adjustment period you may drop courses with no academic penalty. The permanent record will indicate a W for that course, indicating "withdrawn." A charge may be assessed for courses dropped or added during this period, however.

But before you have to worry about dropping or adding classes — before classes even begin — you may have to deal with another concern: your first break with home.

REVIEW FOR CHAPTER 4

1. How do you plan to finance a college education?

2. How much money will you need?

3. How much of your education will your parents pay for, and how much must you pay?

4. What has been done to line up the financing of your education? If you have done nothing, when do you plan to start?

5. Are you interested in any of the alternative ways to earn degree credit? If so, what alternatives do you plan to investigate?

6. Abbreviations to remember:

CLEP	College Level Examination Program
PEP	Proficiency Exam Program

ACT	American College Testing Program
CPEP	College Proficiency Examinations Program
REDE	Regents External Degree Examinations
CAEL	Cooperative Assessment of Experimental Learning

CHAPTER FIVE

Your First Break With Home

"When we drove down the strip, I spotted the fabled 'Vous [Rendezvous]' and 'The Grill.' We pulled on to the campus and it seemed like it went on and on. My mind was boggled by the sheer size. Nowhere had I ever seen so many kids my age concentrated in one place! I remember thinking, *How on earth will I find my away around? Will I fit into the system? Will I be accepted?*"

This was the reaction of one 17-year-old high school student when he was first introduced to the University of Maryland campus which has student population 37,000. As I talked with this student and others, I began to sense that the concerns of the new student and those of the parent are quite different. Likewise, the concerns of the senior are different from those of the new student.

I find that the perspective of parents, pastors, and youth workers differs from that of the new student mainly in that adult concerns are more philosophical than practical. I don't mean to say that a parent's concern over the possibility of sexual involvement, drinking or drugs is not practical. But most often parents and other Christian adults approach these problems intellectually. They seem to think that knowing the truth and being indoctrinated correctly is going to win the day for the new student on the college campus.

FITTING IN

If you are like most students, you probably will be more concerned with fitting into the system than with moral or spiritual seduction. At first you will be preoccupied with matters like, "Where is my dorm room located? How do I find my classes? Will I have enough time to get from one class to the next? Where do I eat?" Once these practical matters are taken care of, you will be ready to give consideration to safeguarding your faith. Let me offer a checklist of some practical matters you should investigate and plan for long before you enter college.

1. *Financial needs. Budget.* Once you have received the financial assistance you have applied for, you will need to develop a financial plan. Your budget should indicate where your money for school is coming from (parents, loan, scholarship, part-time job) and how it is to be spent (tuition, room, board, fees, books, supplies, spending allowance, clothing, laundry and cleaning expenses, transportation, insurance, tithe, gifts, etc.).

Checking Account. You should never carry large sums of money with you, and you should not leave it in your room. You will need a checking account. If your math classes have not taught you how to write checks and balance a checkbook, ask your parents or another adult. You should also be aware that there are several kinds of checking accounts, and that some even offer interest on minimum amounts. Ask the bank to help you select the type of account that is best for you. Another thing you will need to remember is that banks will not let you draw on checks made out to you until they are honored by the issuing bank. This could take up to three weeks (or longer!) for out-of-state checks!

2. *Insurance needs.* Are you covered by any health plan? Do you have an identification card with the plan information on it, in the event you become ill? If insurance papers must be filled out, do you have several sets available in case you need them? Who will be paying for the premiums and when?

Do your parents have a life insurance policy on you? If not, you should discuss with them the possibility of purchasing one.

If you have your own car and are permitted to have it

on campus, is your insurance up-to-date? Who must pay the insurance premium, and when?

3. *Transportation.* How will you get around campus? Is there a bus system? If so, obtain copies of the bus route and the schedule. Are there discounts for students? If so, how do you get them? How about transportation to and from home? Who pays—you or your parents? How often will you return home? If you are allowed to have a car on campus, what are the restrictions? Do you need a special parking sticker? How much does it cost?

4. *Mail.* You will need to give your parents and friends your mailing address and phone number, including area code and zip code.Remember that letter-writing works two ways, and that you should write home from time to time. A post card saying you're alive and well is better than nothing. Plan to take a supply of postcards and stamps and some note paper and envelopes. The post office has pre-stamped envelopes and post cards which can save you a little money. You might want to pre-address a number of postcards, then drop a line once a week.

5. *Your Social Security Number.* Your social security number will be needed on countless forms, and you will be asked for it again and again. Unfortunately, this will be your only identity on some campuses. One student was told she did not exist because the computer had lost her social security number.

6. *Meals.* How are your food needs provided for? Is there a cafeteria on campus? Is it part of your contract with the school? Do you provide your own? Are you allowed to cook in your room? If not, can you have a small hot plate for coffee, tea, and instant soup? Who pays for your food—you or your parents? How much do you need to allow in your budget?

7. *Room Furnishings.* Do you need to provide your own lamp, desk, bookshelf, or curtains? Do you need to supply your own towels and bed linens? Try to get a good look at your room before you move in so you can anticipate what you will need.

8. *Maps and Schedules.* Do you know where everything is located on campus? You will want to get a good map of the campus and find where you go for orientation, for class and to eat. Locate also the library and bookstore. Take a walking tour and locate these places before you even start school. It will also give you an opportunity to test the transportation system. You should know when to be at orientation and class, so keep your schedule readily available. Don't be afraid to ask questions. Everyone else feels just as awkward and out of place as you do. Do them a favor and break the ice by asking.

9. *Health.* I list this separately because a large portion of students drop out of school in their first year because of poor health. Mom isn't around to take care of you now. Watch out for strep throat, staph infections and ear infections particularly; they simply won't go away without medication. If you don't get medical attention, these can develop into secondary complications that may put you to bed for a long time, and maybe out of school for the rest of the year. Your health unit should have literature on basic health care that you should be aware of.

10. *Personal Hygiene.* Hopefully you have learned that you should bathe or shower at least once a day and put on clean underwear after each bath. When mother insisted on these things at home, she wasn't being compulsive. It's a matter of germs, parasites and social embarrassment. Brushing and flossing your teeth after meals is important, too. Don't forget to see your dentist twice a year.

11. *Laundry.* One student who seemed proud of his lack of personal hygiene said that he knew it was time to wash his shirt when he threw it against the wall and it stuck. A clean shirt or blouse each day is not too much to ask for. In cold weather you *might* get two days wear. But better to be on the safe side.

"The Laundry Fairy" used to pick up your dirty clothes and return them to closet and drawer clean and pressed, doing your own laundry will be new to you. The laundry fairy doesn't live at college. Be sure that you include laundry and cleaning expenses in your budget. You also will need to have the right change for commercial washers and dryers.

If laundry seems an unlikely problem to you, consider this true story. A troubled student was referred to the counseling center at the University of Maryland, suffering from acute depression. The counselor quickly discovered the reason for the depression. The young man had run out of clean clothes and did not know how to use a washing machine! The counselor, suspecting that he was being "put on," suggested that the student simply throw away all his dirty clothes and buy new ones. At that the young man revealed the seriousness of the problem. He burst into tears and sobbed, "I can't! I don't know my underwear size!"

Be sure you know what kind of clothes are worn at your school in terms of what is popular and what is essential for the climate. Rainwear and an umbrella will be needed in almost every location. A trunk with a lock is important, and you may want a standing clothes locker with a lock. One of the problems living with other students is that they borrow your things—everything from bandaids to blouses. It's not that they're dishonest. "Thoughtless" is the word. Mom isn't there to provide everything, so they tend to rely on others to meet their needs. Don't let others borrow; it doesn't help them learn responsibility.

After the initial "outfitting" for college, who is responsible for your clothing needs—you or your parents? Do you know your clothing and shoe sizes?

12. *What to pack.* Here is a partial list of some of the items you may need to take with you, in addition to clothing:

Linens	Toilet Articles	Study Aids
pillow	soap	dictionary
sheets	toothpaste	dictionary
pillow case	mouthwash	desk lamp
blankets	deodorant	typewriter
bedspread	dental floss	calculator
towels	toothbrush	thesaurus
washcloths	hair care items	notebooks
hot water bottle	make up/shaving items	paper, pens, etc.

Health Care Items	Room Furnishings	Laundry Items
aspirin	alarm clock	laundry soap
thermometer	extension cord	fabric softener
bandaids	3-way plug or adapter	iron
first aid cream	hot plate	hangers
tissues	desk	laundry basket
vitamins	bookshelves	liquid soap for
Misc.	curtains	delicate hand-
umbrella	trunk	washables
postcards, stamps	standing clothes	coins for commercial
address book	locker	washers, dryers

This should be enough to alert you to the practical concerns that you will face. For further suggestions, read *Introduction to Dorm Living* by Mildred Z. Ward[1] and *College Knowledge.*[2] For health care, see the excellent booklet called "Help Yourself."[3]

LIVING AWAY FROM HOME

If you are going to live away from home, you need to decide what kind of living arrangement you are going to make. There are several possibilities, but most students select one of three major choices: dormitory, fraternity or sorority house, or Christian house.

Dormitory Life. Dorm life has both positive and negative features. Convenience to classrooms and campus facilities such as the gym and tennis courts are frequently mentioned by students as positive features. Others mention such advantages as meeting new people and having the library to study at. One student said, "Whenever I go home on weekends I never get around to studying. I do better if I stay on campus and go to the library to study."

Not everyone is as positive, however. Small rooms, high cost and a lack of privacy are frequently mentioned. "The walls are paper thin," reported one student. "Loud talking and music keep me from concentrating on my studies." Women frequently cite the rising crime rate as a matter of concern. One girl said, "The parking lots on campus simply aren't safe. Mugging, exhibitionism and rape are common fears among the girls."

At first, loneliness and shyness can be a problem, but if you are going to live in a dorm, you can take the initiative. Recalling her days in the dorm, Sue said, "Before I left for school my first year, a very wise friend took me aside and said, 'Sue, everybody's going to be as lonely as you are the first week. Reach out. Everyone else needs you just as much as you need them.'"

"I went down to every room and said, 'Hi. My name's Sue.' The response was tremendous. And we all got together and did something dumb like seeing how many people we could throw into the fountain in front of the administration building. That was one of our favorite things for the rest of the year.

"The important thing to realize is that they were not Christians, but I was able to set a positive moral tone. I wanted to make the reputation for myself as a person who knew how to have good, clean fun. I was always organizing something. Brooms and ping pong balls make great equipment for a hockey game! It's important that Christians not be whimps or nerds. No one wants to be with a dud. This is why I think drinking is so popular on the campus. It lowers the inhibitions. When the others would go out to drink, I'd order a Coke. When they'd ask, I just said I'd rather have a Coke. They accepted it. My father died an alcoholic, so I didn't have much interest in drinking. But my message to the Christian living in the dorm is to *initiate* and *be creative*. Get out there and give them some alternative to booze. And I don't mean just Bible study. I mean good, clean fun!"

The Christian House. Dave had flunked out of the university during his sophomore year because partying and girl-chasing caught up with him. Even though he was a Christian, he made choices that caused him to lose valuable time at school. He went to a junior college to elevate his grade point average, and then returned to the University of Maryland. When he returned, he realized that his former living arrangements had been a major factor in his failure the first time. He had come to school wanting to chase girls and to drink; the guys in his living unit had facilitated it.

This time, he decided to live in a Christian House—a house that is rented by a group of Christians or by a Christian organization that leases it to Christian students.

Dave said, "It doesn't matter how strong you are in Christ. You can get worn down by getting in with the wrong bunch. That's what happened in my situation. I really saw the need for Christian brothers after I flunked out. Living with them, I feel more secure in Christ. When I'm out on the campus I know who I am. I'm a man who believes in Jesus Christ, and I know who He is. I'm not so easily influenced by what others say. I'm not scared to speak up."

Today Dave draws a lot of strength from the Christian guys he lived with.

The student who is interested in this kind of living arrangement should contact the various Christian organizations on campus to find out what is available. This is something that can be done as soon as you choose which school you plan to attend. You might even run an ad in the campus newspaper stating your need for housing with other "born again Christian students" or an ad with language so encoded as to reach those of like faith.

Fraternity and Sorority Houses. The "Greek" system (from Greek letters that comprise the names of many fraternities and sororities) provides an opportunity for students to live and socialize with a usually cohesive group of friends. Because a member of a fraternity or sorority often lives in the same house for three or four years, he or she is sometimes able to develop longer-lasting relationships than are students in dormitories where the student population can change yearly.

On some campuses, the Greeks offer a wider variety of social activities than do the residence halls. On others, though, the residence hall systems are highly organized and students tend to stick with the same dorm for three or four years. In either case, a Christian student should especially consider two factors when choosing a living unit: 1) his or her own spiritual strength and need for fellowship in a living unit; 2) his or her potential for ministering to members of the living unit.

Many fraternities and sororities were founded on Christian or quasi-Christian principles. Though Greeks have often unfortunately received bad reputations for hazing, alcohol abuse, and drug abuse, many of the national organizations are making concerted efforts to counter those trends. Some have made major strides. If the Christian student is fairly strong as a believer and has good spiritual support from a Christian fellowship on campus, he or she could have a strategic ministry among the members of the fraternity or sorority. On many campuses the Greeks have Bible studies in their houses. Living and working in close relationships with non-Christian students can provide a great opportunity for witness through one's life and words.

Of course, in any living situation, there can be pressures to conform. Students who are not well-grounded spiritually should be cautious about entering a living situation — Greek or independent (non-Greek) — that would drag them down spiritually. At the very least they should seek out a good Christian fellowship, for the challenges to one's faith can be great, indeed.

I found this out in the Air Force as a new young Christian. I lived in barracks with sixty other men who had a need to prove they were macho and that Christians were wimps. My convictions were severely tested, but a positive and consistent stand never failed to win the respect of my buddies. I always made it my first task to find other Christians in my barracks or in the squadron. We drew a lot of strength from each other.

Living at Home. Some campuses, particularly state universities, are commuter campuses. Many of the students live at home and commute to school. There are distinct advantages to this. Cost of living at home is less. You enjoy all the amenities of home life such as the convenience of a washer and dryer and having your own room. You are also able to maintain many of the social contacts you made in high school. But there are disadvantages as well, both for parent and student.

Disadvantages of Living At Home. The major disadvantage to living at home is the inevitable conflict that arises between parent and child. The child feels that he's old enough to run his own life and should be free to come and go as he wishes. The lifestyle of the young, single student is also quite different from that of the middle-age parent who goes to bed after the ten o'clock news and gets up at dawn.

It's not unusual for the single student to come in from a date at midnight, spend the next hour getting ready for a ski trip the next day, and then bang around until five o'clock the next morning before heading off to ski.

Or, suppose he discovers after studying until midnight that he has no clean jeans for school the next day. So he decides to do a washer full of clothes. This is bound to blow up into something ugly, and I guarantee that a parent-child discussion over the "reasonableness" of washing clothes at midnight will yield nothing. Why? Because what is reasonable to an energetic, 18-year-old teenager is not reasonable to a 50-year-old with hypertension.

Successful family living demands a sacrifice on the part of all who live under the same roof. It is a sacrifice that takes into consideration the lifestyle and needs of everyone in the household—both the need to sleep and the need to wash clothes. Too often neither the student nor the parents are willing to make that kind of sacrifice.

The student feels, "I'm an adult now and I'm going to run my life the way I want." The parent often feels, "I've sacrificed for the past 18 years and I'm tired of it. When do I get my turn to enjoy a bit of life?" How on earth is it possible, then, for the student and parents to live together successfully?

Coping With the Disadvantages. If you are going to live at home, you must realize that there is no total freedom when people live together as a family. Because of the mutual concern each has for the other, certain accountability is expected. It's perfectly reasonable for your parents to want to know where you are going and when you expect to be back. Your parents have a responsibility to give the same consideration to you when they go out. When you live together as a family, you must care about each other in order for there to be harmony. And if you care, accountability puts to rest any worry over members of the family who are absent.

It's also reasonable for your parents to set certain house rules as to curfew. Young men and women often don't understand why their parents can't go to bed and not worry about when or if they will come home. But look at it this way.

For 18 years your parents have trained themselves to be aware of any distress or problem you might have. From my own experience I know that for 18 years we parents sleep with one ear open at night to listen for a bronchitis attack or other sounds of distress from a sick child. When the child gets older, starts using the family car, and dates, we stay up to make sure he gets home and to bed okay. When he reaches age 18 we just don't turn it off. We find that we can't go to sleep until he's home and settled in for the night. And we find that we're still alert to sounds in the night and can't sleep until we're sure that everything's all right.

It's reasonable that certain hours be declared quiet hours for sleeping. TV and music is turned low enough so as not to bother those who want to sleep. And if it does, they use earplugs or you use earphones.

Laundry is not done at midnight. Living together means planning ahead to do your laundry at the convenience of others, not just yourself. *Adults living under the same roof are not independent.*

Another common source of conflict is over student messiness at home. Is your shared family area such as kitchen, family room, den and living room often strewn with your books, sweaters, papers, dishes, glasses, bottles and assorted litter, not always identifiable? Is your room in worse shape? The confusion of rumpled and strewn bed linen, clothes hanging out of half-closed dresser drawers and a closet that can't be shut because it looks like an overflowing Salvation Army clothing deposit bin add to conflicts with parents.

My wife and I have pretty much given up the battle for the bedroom. We just ask that the sheets be changed once a week and a skip-loader be driven in to shovel out the room. We do insist, however, that everyone be responsible for cleaning up his own mess in the shared family areas. Dishes and glasses are rinsed and put into the dish washer, and mom runs it when it's full. Personal articles are put away. The bathroom is likewise picked up and wiped up.

Your parents should not have to argue with you over the reasonableness of these expectations. These are the terms necessary for successful family living. All should agree on them and remind each other of that agreement. This is the nature of family living.

NEED FOR PARENTS' SUPPORT

No matter where the student lives, at home, dorm, Christian house, fraternity or sorority house, the moral support of parents is important. By that I mean the student needs to know that the parent is there and is interested in what happens.

Because a great deal of misunderstanding goes on between parents and college students, I am addressing this section to both you and your parents. It would be wise to ask your parents to read it, and then to discuss it with you.

One of the major problems parents face is the growing independence of their children. As I pointed out earlier, changing habits that have formulated over 18 years is not an easy task. Added to that is the impression that the student no longer needs his parents.

One parent expressed the pain of this frustration by saying, "After all, whatever advice I give is seldom followed or my son acts like I am butting in. And I never get any letters or phone calls. I don't believe my son is really interested in home or parents, except when it comes to money."

The student often does feel that the parent is butting in

or is using financial aid as a lever to get his own way. This is especially true with a commuter school like the University of Maryland. Many of the students either live at home and commute or live close enough to home that they could go every weekend. A lot of time parents don't understand that the student needs to develop his own social life. What may appear to be less interest in the family may in reality be the result of the student's developing his own life at school. Many students feel pressure to be involved with family life even though they'd rather be doing something else or may have to study.

Parents must realize that in our culture the age span between 18 and 25 is one in which the student needs to learn to establish himself as an independent adult. He could be crippled socially by well-meaning parents who in the name of love and family keep him from doing this. Once the student becomes a secure adult in his own right, he can be part of the family system as an *adult* and not a child.

Dave's Story. Remember Dave, who had to drop out of school because partying and girl-chasing caused him to flunk out in his sophomore year? I asked him how his parents might have helped him avoid what he went through. Dave replied, "I really lacked friendship with my parents — I didn't think they were really interested in what was going on in my life. Not that I was asking them to butt in, but I just wanted to know that they care. It was hard to say, 'Hey, Dad. I'm doing real bad.' Or, 'Dad. I shouldn't be doing this or that.' Dad really couldn't support me because he didn't know what was going on in my life. Being a friend to your kid, supporting him emotionally, not butting in, but letting him know what's coming, that's what I mean. Tell your kid that you know beer and girls will be available, that you know he can stay up as late as he wants and do anything he wants, answering to no one. Just let him know what's going to happen if he's not careful."

Parents seem to have difficulty in mastering this, however. It usually comes across as butting in. I suggest to parents that they say to their teenager something like this:

"Hey, Dave, I've got something on my mind I need to talk about. You don't have to talk about it if you don't want. But would you let me share my concerns with you?" Then the parent talks in terms of *his own* concern. He doesn't come across as though Dave is ignorant of the facts or that Dave will fail.

The student needs to be given the credit for knowing problems exist already and for being able to handle them, whether or not such optimism is warranted. The parent says what he needs to say without insulting the intelligence or integrity of the student. The ego of the 17 and 18-year-old is very delicate. He may not know what he needs to know, but his ego can't afford to let you discover that. Respect his ego need when you talk to him, and show him your friendship.

Sue's Experience. Sue, a recent graduate, had this to say.

"Parents need to be involved with their college kids right from the beginning. When your son or daughter sends away applications to colleges, ask questions like, 'What is it you like about that school? What do you want in that school?' I'm talking about *being available.*

"I feel like I got misplaced in my family. I couldn't go to mom or other parent figures because they didn't seem to be interested. Then I finally decided to take the initiative. It meant horrendous phone bills, but I started calling mom and saying, 'Hey, this happened at school.' The response was, 'Really?' *I got a reaction!* It was great. She wanted to know all about it. She became involved.

"Too often the kids would go off to school, come home on weekends, but there was no in-depth talk. The family would watch TV and eat together, but there was no involvement below the superficial level. But where there is involvement between the two — that's what kept me straight a lot of times. Some time of involvement was part of the friendship. An active part.

"A parent can be involved but still let the student be responsible. I need to be responsible for myself. But it's nice to have the parent there to lick the wounds or share in the joy. It gives you a sense of security to feel that they are behind you when you are away at school."

Knowing that parents support you and are interested in you is not enough, however. Whether the campus is in Maryland, California, Alabama or Virginia; whether it's a Christian student or leader talking, I hear the same thing again and again. The student entering college needs Christian fellowship.

THE NEED FOR CHRISTIAN FELLOWSHIP

Let me hasten to add that not just any Christian fellowship will do. It's important that the fellowship be compatible with your personality and temperament.

Dave, whom I mentioned earlier, was turned off at his first attempt to find fellowship. "They turned me off because they acted like Christians are supposed to be studying the Bible or witnessing all the time. They didn't know how to have fun."

Sue felt the same way. "My needs go beyond Bible study. I have a need for *social* relations with people. As human beings we are social creatures. The Bible makes it clear that we can glorify God in our eating and drinking—our social life—as well as in witnessing."

It's important that you contact Christian groups on campus and get acquainted with the people long before you leave home. Three major groups that work on most campuses are Campus Crusade, Intervarsity Christian Fellowship, and Navigators. Each of the groups has its own approach and tends to attract a different type of student.

I asked Phares Wood, Senior Campus Crusade Woman at the University of Maryland, to comment on the difference of philosophy and approach of these organizations.

"All three have the same goal with different emphasis. Intervarsity would stress the intellectual side of the spiritual life. They offer a strong apologetic [defense of the faith] approach to Christianity. This is why their emphasis is their books, especially Frances Schaeffer's writings. They will have discussion groups on such topics as abortion and pro life, things that hit the political and spiritual life of the student. Navigators is most similar to Crusade, but their great emphasis is on discipleship. They look for a strong commitment from all the people who associate with them. They do have groups for people just starting out that would be the equivalent of Campus Crusade's First Step Discovery Group, but they expect to see people go on.

"Crusade attracts many different people, and we try to have a place for everyone. We try to deal with each person at the level of commitment 'we find them."

How do students find these groups? Parents can help you. Ask them to spend a weekend on campus with you before you enter college. Do it while it's in session so you can get a feel for campus life. Hunt down the leaders of the various Christian organizations. Talk with them. Get to know some of the students in the organizations. Get names, addresses, and phone numbers so when you arrive on campus you will have some people to contact. But above all, find a group that suits your personality and temperament. Remember that an 18-year-old is socially a very needy person. The group's social compatibility with you is as important as its doctrinal purity.

Don't neglect off-campus fellowship at local churches. Many Christian groups on campus see themselves as *arms* of the local church, not substitutes for it. A strong church experience, with solid Biblical teaching and fellowship with Christians of all ages, is vital to your spiritual growth.

Many churches adjacent to campus offer excellent activities for Christian college kids. You also have an opportunity to meet people not connected with the campus. Fellowship away from campus can be a relief from the crowding, and academic and social pressures you feel. Get to know the churches in your area. Get acquainted with the church families, and take advantage of the opportunity for social and spiritual involvement with them.

And don't be afraid to let the people you live with know that you're a Christian. Don't be arrogant, self-righteous or

obnoxious about it, but by letting others know, you have
the best chance of finding other Christians to socialize with.
The more Christians you meet, the more chance you have to
know what's going on. You will soon discover a network of
Christians throughout the campus, each with its own group
that appeals to a particular personality and temperament.
Some will be quite regimented. Others will be more social
and fun-loving.

Here's where Dave got off on the wrong foot when he
began college. To him, being a Christian was a very relaxed
way of life. He was fun-loving and not too serious. He
wasn't ready for the group he met first. They were very
serious-minded and were either in Bible study or witnessing.
He wanted to go out and play basketball, but he had no
takers. When his other friends played ball with him and provided for his social needs, he began to drift.

Taking a positive stand as a Christian also offers a
measure of protection. Yes, you will be tested. Your dorm-
mates don't want a hypocrite around. But if they see that
you're genuine, they will respect your convictions and not
try to compromise you. What is more, once you've taken a
stand as a Christian, you don't dare backslide. You'll never
hear the end of it from the unbelievers you live with!

The question of relating with unbelievers — especially on a
university campus — is a complex one. What *is* the place of
the Christian on the secular campus?

REVIEW FOR CHAPTER 5

1. What is your social security number (without looking)? If you don't know it, memorize it.

2. What will you do in the event of a major illness, and
you find you can't take care of yourself?

3. Do you have hospitalization coverage?

4. Do your parents (or friends) think your personal
hygiene is adequate?

5. Do you feel the interest and support of your parents?

6. Where do you plan to live when you go to college?

7. If you plan to live at home, do you understand the "house rules" — what is expected of you at home?

8. When do you and your parents intend to contact a campus Christian fellowship? If it has not yet been done, when will it be done?

9. Do you have any reservations about the people on campus knowing you are a Christian?

10. What churches adjacent to the campus do your parents and you feel might provide off-campus fellowship? If this is not known, when will you find out?

CHAPTER SIX

We And They: The Christian
On The Secular Campus

I told a number of Christian students and Christian leaders on campus that I was writing a book to help prepare Christians for an education on a secular campus. One of the chapters would be called, "We and They: The Christian On the Secular Campus." What could they tell me about their experience as Christians on a secular campus?

Some responded very positively to the chapter title. "Yes, *we* must be careful. *They* may corrupt us." Others were more negative. They felt that the we/they approach stereotyped the unbeliever — the secularist — as the corruptor of Christian morals.

I had deliberately put the question that way to see what kind of reaction I would get. Though I never have taken any kind of poll, I have become aware over the years that Christians tend to react to unbelievers in one of two ways: 1) We have nothing in common with the unbeliever. He is the enemy of God. Any meaningful contact is achieved only in Christ; 2) We have a great deal in common with the unbeliever. That commonality provides the basis of a working relationship with him and a basis of witness to him.

To understand the place of the Christian on the secular campus we must deal with the question, "Do we have anything in common?" This will affect the way we live, study, and socialize with the unbeliever and the way we witness to him. But before we can evaluate our commonality, we must first dispel some myths.

Many of these myths came up in a counseling session with a family who disagreed about where the son should attend college. The son preferred going to an in-state secular college where his friends went, but he felt he had little to say in the matter since his parents were paying his way. Dad sided with the son. He felt that the college was educationally solid. Its rules offered support to the morality they had taught their son. And there was plenty of opportunity for Christian fellowship.

Mother was adamant. A secular college would corrupt her son's morals and intellectually seduce him into thinking in the way of the world. She said, "The unbeliever's views are completely wrong. The Bible says that he is blind to the truth. How can we learn anything from someone who is blind to the truth? Secular colleges offer the wisdom of man. Our reliance should be on Christ and the wisdom that comes from Him. You don't get that in a secular college. Secular college education is not only taught by unbelievers, but it is designed also to appeal to the unbeliever. What fellowship does darkness have with light?"

The mother's arguments reveal a number of myths about the unbeliever and secular education. Let me identify and correct them:

Myth #1. "The unbeliever's views are completely wrong." This is not entirely true. Psalm 19:1-2 makes it clear that God speaks through nature. His glory and his work are clearly revealed. Not only are they revealed, but Romans 1:18-23 makes it clear that they are also understood. The plain declaration is that they *did* know him but chose not to honor him or give thanks. *Man's great sin is ingratitude.* He knows but will not acknowledge that he knows. This is why God can hold all men accountable for rejecting him. It isn't that they do not know him; they do know, but they are determined to supress that truth (Romans 1:18).

Myth #2. "The unbeliever is blind to the truth. How can we learn anything from someone who is blind to the truth?" I Corinthians 2:14-15 is usually cited to support this view. A careful examination of the passage reveals, however, that the unbeliever (the "natural man") cannot understand *the things of the Spirit of God.* Theologian Charles Hodge makes a distinction between "the things of the Spirit" and "things external." He says, "Inability is asserted only in reference to the things of the Spirit. Unregenerated men are able to perform moral acts. They are able also to understand the things that are external. Inability has to do with the things of God. These are the things of the Spirit, things connected with salvation."[1]

The unbeliever, through natural revelation, is able to understand the great scientific and moral principles upon which God has built His creation. The tragedy is that he is unwilling to acknowledge God as the author and finisher of that work. Or, if he does acknowledge a god, that god is but a mere shadow of the glorious God of the Bible.

Myth #3. "Secular college teaches the wisdom of man." This statement mixes fiction with fact. If "wisdom of man" means theories of the universe's origin and the ultimate end, then I would agree. Without understanding the God of the Bible, no scientist can deduce where it came from and where it is going or the meaning behind it all. If "the wisdom of man" refers to the unbeliever's ability to teach us *how* God's creation works, including everything from chemistry to the dynamics of interpersonal relations, then I cannot agree.

Unbelievers, as creatures made in the image of God, have a God-given intelligence to understand how this creation works. We may not agree on why it works as it does or where it will all end. But together we can learn a great deal about the how.

Myth #4. "Our reliance should be on Christ and the wisdom that comes from Him. You don't get this in a secular college." It's true that our reliance is to be on Christ. But it is not true that Christ and education in a secular institution are antithetical. Historically, God has used such institutions to train His hand-picked leaders. Moses and Daniel are just two examples. God uses unbelievers to accomplish his work in this world. It is true that unbelieving men oppose him. But they are limited in how far they can go. This is what common grace is all about. God holds down the evil and promotes the good, even in lost men.

Theologian Cornelius Van Til offers the illustration of a

mutiny on a ship.[2] A creature called Lucifer gets the crew of the ship to mutiny against the Captain. Though they mutiny and take over the ship, they cannot remove the Captain from the bridge. The Captain continues the ship on its course, and the mutineers, if they are to survive, must keep the ship functioning. They must continue to distill fresh drinking water, keep the steam up in the boilers and feed themselves. One day the ship will reach its destination and the mutineers will be dealt with then. In the meantime, even though they are in rebellion against the Captain, they dare not jeopardize the safety of the ship. They must continue to exercise those skills they know so well or they will perish.

It is true that the world of unbelieving men are in rebellion against God. But as long as they are passengers on this planet earth, they had better be very careful how they behave. Even these rebels recognize that the only way they will survive is to use this planet carefully and productively and to hold down mindless anarchy. Even in rebellion there is government, education, and the production of goods and services. God is determined that man will do at least this much. This was the cultural mandate given in Genesis 1:28. Even though man fell, that mandate still is in force.

God not only works through unbelievers but also through "second causes." He does not mystically and directly involve himself in all that he accomplishes. He uses unbelievers and principles of good husbandry to make sure this planet survives to the day of reckoning. Believers can and must work with unbelievers side by side because we have our mutual well-being at stake. We must fill the earth and bring it under our control (Genesis 1:28).

What causes these myths to be so pervasive among believers? Although many Christians are devoted Bible students, I have found that many perpetuate these myths as well as downright error simply because they are *doctrinally illiterate.* They are therefore unable to relate successfully to unbelievers professionally, socially, and their witness often suffers because of it. They come across as harsh, unfriendly and remote.

What can be done to correct this problem? I think we need to review our understanding of a number of doctrines we have tended to neglect, in order to grasp the truth and avoid error. I have selected several doctrines to consider.

1. *Sovereignty of God.* God is king and still is on His throne. Though Satan and the unbeliever are in rebellion against Him, He still is in control of His world. He has not abandoned it and is even using unbelievers to accomplish His purposes in it.

2. *Man the Image of God.* Man was created as a personality, a reflection of God, with intellect, emotion and will. The exercise of these elements of personality are part of his heritage as a *man.* For this reason our *humanness* is to be valued.

3. *The Fall.* The fall is to be seen in two dimensions: vertical (ethical) and horizontal (metaphysical). Man fell ethically. That is, his vertical relation with God was broken beyond man's ability to repair it. If the relationship is to be repaired, God must intervene in special grace to restore it. Horizontally, in relation to other men and creation, man remains intact. Even after the fall man is still declared to be the image of God (Genesis 9:6; 1 Corinthians 11:7; James 3:9). The recreation passages (Colossians 3:9-10; 2 Corinthians 3:18; Ephesians 4:24) should be understood in the ethical sense. By being saved a man does not become more of a man. He always enjoyed that quality as a creature made in God's image. If this were not so, we could kill unbelievers with no penalty because they do not enjoy the status of "image of God."

4. *Common Grace.* Van Til, writing in his book *Common Grace,* says that the sinner is enabled to make "a certain positive accomplishment in history because of God's gifts to him" (Psalm 145:9; Luke 6:35-36; Acts 14:16-17; 1 Timothy 4:10). Because of God's grace the unbeliever is able to enjoy health and happiness and is able to function creatively and bring the world under control. It is man's rejection of common grace that heightens his guilt (Romans

1:18-23; 2:14-15). It is also the work of God that holds down evil in the world.

5. *Natural Revelation.* This is that work of God whereby He reveals His person and work through His creation (Psalm 19:1-2; Romans 1 & 2; Acts 14:16-17).

6. *Human Ability and Responsibility.* Unbelieving human beings, because of the previous truths, are able to accomplish a great deal of good, productive work. It is the natural outgrowth of their humanness, which is a reflection of God's image. Not only are they able, they also are responsible.

Christians likewise are able and responsible to function as creatures made in God's image. Having exhausted the benefits of the fruit of their first birth, they can rest with confidence on the benefits of their second birth. Or, to put it another way, the benefits of special grace in the saving work of Christ do not replace the benefits of common grace and our inheritance of God's image in our humanity. The Christian is twice blessed in grace. He enjoys the benefits of both common and special grace.

7. *Dualism.* This is an ancient error that draws a false antithesis between the spiritual (or heavenly) and the material (or earthly). The truth is that God is the God of both.

8. *Mysticism and Asceticism.* The error of dualism tends to promote the errors of mysticism and asceticism. Mysticism is that tendency to seek God solely through spiritual or other than earthly means, such as Bible study, prayer and meditation. These are proper exercises but are not the only channels through which God is reached. Asceticism is the tendency to deny human comfort and anything earthly with the belief that such denial will help achieve a more spiritual frame of mind. Monasticism is an example.

9. *Cultural Mandate.* Understanding that God intends us to carry out Genesis 1:28 helps us to see the spiritual value of work other than evangelism. It also helps us to appreciate the place of the unbeliever in the task of controlling the

world and working more effectively with him.[3]

10. *Humanism.* In dealing with *secular* humanism where man is the measure of all things, there is a danger of losing sight of *Christian* humanism where our humanity is to be valued as a reflection of God's image. We need to consider just what we mean by the word *secular.*

SECULARISM

sec-u-lar 1. a) of or relating to worldly things as distinguished from things sacred or religious; temporal; worldly *(secular music, secular schools).*

This dictionary definition of secular does point up the fact that secular is a useful word in helping us to make some distinctions. But in the final analysis, there is no such thing as secular. God is still king of the universe. He has not abandoned His world to Satan and the unbeliever, and no one can escape from His love:

Where can I go from Thy Spirit?
Or where can I flee from Thy presence?
If I ascend to heaven, Thou art there;
If I make my bed in Sheol, behold, Thou art there.
If I take the wings of the dawn,
If I dwell in the remotest part of the sea,
Even there Thy hand will lead me,
And Thy right hand will lay hold of me.
If I say, "Surely the darkness will overwhelm me,
And the light around me will be the night,"
Even the darkness is not dark to Thee,
And the night is as bright as the day.
Darkness and light are alike to Thee (Psalm 139:7-12).

In common grace, He holds down evil and promotes the good. In reality, Satan and the unbeliever are working on borrowed Christian capital, as Van Til would put it.

This is important to grasp. Too often Christians on the secular college campus carry the we/they antithesis to an unscriptural extreme *(we* must be careful; *they* may corrupt us).

To some extent that caution is in order, as I have said

throughout this book. Christian fellowship and testimony are important. But what we must not do is become an exclusive club with the idea that "they" work "their" side of the street and "we" work "our" side. The fact of the matter is that *God owns both sides of the street.* I'm not going to act obnoxious or self-righteous about it, but I can go anywhere I want on the block with the confidence that I'm one of the king's kids and my daddy owns it all! It is this kind of relaxed confidence that enables us to be in the world and winsome, yet not of the world.

Here is where the salt meets the earth. I understand Jesus' illustration (Matthew 5:13) to refer to salt's ability to hold down corruption. We can't hold down corruption unless we are where the corruption is.

Now I realize that there is a "secularist" attitude and a move toward "secularism" wherein a conscious effort is being made to remove all traces of God. But I have to smile at the idea of getting rid of God. I don't think that he is as worried about his demise as we are. In fact, the psalmist says that God is having a good chuckle over it all. God laughs at those who take a stand against him, and one day he shall terrify them with his fury (Psalm 2:1-5)!

In the meantime, let's not be shaken. Let's act as though we believe that He's on the throne waiting for His time to put down the rebellion. While we wait we have to live and work among the rebels. We may even go to school with them. And while we do, we hope they'll get the message that there's no such thing as secular. Though unbelievers may deny it, it is in God that all men live and move and exist (Acts 17:28). We want to love them and help them understand this through faith in Christ.

THE SEDUCTION OF THE MIND

I don't mean to imply by what I've said that we need not be concerned about the intellectual seduction of Christian students. Indeed, we must. But I have said all this to help you understand what we must do to keep it from happening.

If you allow yourself to believe the notion that unbelievers are at best unhappy, unfulfilled, uninformed people — and at worst, two-headed monsters stalking you and waiting to seduce you — you will be in big trouble when you go off to college. Yes, you will meet many rebels and losers; but you will meet a lot of beautiful people, too — unsaved students and unbelieving faculty members. As you live, work and study with these people, you will discover many unbelievers are very happy, very fulfilled and very informed.

If you come from a church or home setting where the Christians are not particularly lovely people but uptight, legalistic and bigoted, the problem will be accentuated. You will ask yourself, "How come the Christians at home aren't as happy and well-adjusted as these people?"

Because the church is in the business of reaching out to all people, the unlovely as well as the lovely, church youth groups often have a high proportion of unlovely people who are accepted nowhere else. If you go to a secular campus from that kind of youth group, you are bound to make comparisons and wonder why being saved didn't change the nature of those unlovely Christians. You may find the exciting unbelievers on the campus more to your liking.

I say this to make the point that the seduction of the mind does not begin *philosophically*. It begins *socially*. 18-year-olds are throbbing social creatures. If you are like most of them, friendships, fitting into the system, and avoiding social blunders are at the top of your list. Whatever you have learned about truth and error is still there for you to draw on, but it's not your first concern.

When you begin to satisfy your social needs and aspirations with beautiful, exciting unbelievers, you become vulnerable to the seduction of the mind. You are enjoying a lifestyle and an emotional fulfillment you may not have had before. It feels good to be loved and accepted and have fun. Because we *want* to do what feels good to us, we open ourselves to the next step in the seduction: rationalization.

Rationalization is that function of the intellect whereby we justify what we feel like doing. Yes, we may know that the Bible says we shouldn't. But if we want to do it badly enough, we'll find a way to justify it intellectually.

Isn't this what Adam and Eve experienced in Eden? Adam and Eve were to obey God and believe that He had their best interest at heart when He laid down His laws. But when they looked at the forbidden fruit, they saw that it was good for food, a delight to the eyes and desirable to make one wise. The *attractiveness* of the forbidden fruit was the first problem.

The second is that Satan capitalized on it and made Adam and Eve believe that *God didn't have their best interest at heart* and that He was lying. Satan told them that they wouldn't die if they ate. According to Satan God didn't want them to eat because God knew that when they did they would know the difference between good and evil and be like God. So there were two problems: first, the attractiveness of the fruit and second, the feeling that God was keeping something from them. God was a spoil-sport.

As Christians we need to face the fact that knowing the difference between right and wrong is not enough, whether it has to do with philosophy, theology or morality. There must be a relationship between you and God and between you and your parents. You need to be able to trust and respect your parents and God, so you won't feel that they are just out to spoil your fun.

Young adults like you come to believe that the forbidden fruit is not for you either by taking our word for it, and trusting it, or by bitter experience. Which way you go will largely depend on the strength of a loving and caring relationship with God, parent and the church. On campus it will depend on the strength of a loving and caring relationship with other Christians who are fulfilling your social needs to be loved and to belong.

I raised this issue with Sue, Marti and Rhonda. Sue is 23, and a graduate. Rhonda is 21 and a junior, and Marti is 20 and a junior. I asked them what they thought about my theory of the seduction of the mind. They felt it was on target and saw it happen in school.

Rhonda said, "It happens very easily when you have a prof whom you respect and look up to. You find that you begin to respect his views, even though they may be different from your own. It creeps up on you."

Sue agreed. "I saw girls live on every word of the prof. I had an uneasy feeling when I heard them talk, because they seemed to place too much emphasis on what the prof was saying, as though he could speak no wrong. They were believing too easily. Their lack of a healthy, critical mind told me that something else was going on. They were infatuated."

"You also run into this when you see a great looking guy who's not a Christian," Rhonda added. "I have a Christian girlfriend, and we joke about it all the time. We'll see a nice looking guy and I'll say, 'I wonder if he's worth going carnal over.'

"We joke, but I've learned that it's easy to compromise when you run into a nice guy that you really like. It might start out just being good friends and going to classes together. He calls you up and it starts out really innocent. It may start out as a friendly relationship, but it's easy to fall because unsaved guys really can be nice."

Marti added, "That's true. I tend to admire people I can relate to. The personality and the person are both attractive. Then you go on to admiring what they think.

"It happens in small school as well as large ones. I had a summer class. It was a drawing class. My roommate and I both were in it together. Everyone there was so boring, but the teacher was great. He was up there cracking jokes and my roommate and I were the only ones laughing.

"He came over to us. He has a very dynamic personality, very outgoing. He'd sit with us and talk with us. I could be attracted to him just because he had an attractive personality. I could see how easy it would be to move on to respect his opinions and ideas."

That hit a responsive nerve in Sue. "Now that I think

about it, I've taken two summers of courses at Maryland and I've seen the beginnings of that in almost every one of my classes."

I wanted to know what draws believers and unbelievers together. What is the attraction that lays the groundwork for the seduction of the mind and the rationalization? As I continued asking these questions, all three women seemed to agree that people tend to be good friends with those they have similarities with. Sometimes, then, Christians are drawn to non-believers. Socializing becomes complicated because it's easy to say, "Let's go down to the Vous for a few cool ones."

"It takes massive creativity," said Sue, "for a Christian to figure out something fun to do!"

I asked them to tell me what the answer is. Sue replied, "You tell us! I had a long talk with one of the guys at Cornerstone [an off-campus Christian organization] the other night and asked him how you get to know people. I've been to their meetings and so far I know how everybody in the group became a Christian, what fellowships they've been in, how long they've been a Christian, and that type of thing. How do you get beyond that? We spend an hour delving into the question, 'Who are you?' and figuring out ways to initiate more response along that line.

"I think sometimes Christians are just as guilty of not getting to know people as the superficial unsaved people we criticize. I see a lot of similarity between Christian organizations and the wild social functions where everybody's going out drinking. Christians can be superficial without the booze just as much as the others are with the booze. Let's not kid ourselves that *we* have *real* fellowship in Christ. That may be our position because we're in Christ. But that doesn't make it our experience unless we develop it. In college you need people — one way or another. Bible studies are fine, but I need *people* — Christian people to interact with at the gut level."

This is what I came to again and again in my talks with Christian students and leaders on campus — people and the social *impact* they have on the students.

Marti seemed to voice the conclusion of most. She said, "I think that the incoming Christian freshman ought to check out some Christian organizations right away. Find out what's going on in their activities. Then maybe later come back and deal with the non-Christian people around you."

REVIEW FOR CHAPTER 6

1. Does the believer have anything in common with the unbeliever?

2. True or false: When Adam fell into sin, he and all mankind lost the image of God.

3. True or false: When man fell he became totally incapable of restoring fellowship to God by himself.

4. True or false: The unbeliever is able to enjoy health and happiness on earth because God's common grace.

5. True or false: God reveals Himself both through the Bible and in nature.

6. True or false: Unbelievers are able to accomplish a great deal of good, productive work.

7. True or false: Dualism teaches that the material world is evil and the spiritual and immaterial are good.

8. True or false: Mysticism puts an emphasis on the spiritual world rather than the material world.

9. True or false: Asceticism tends to deny human comfort in the belief that such denial makes us more spiritual.

10. True or false: There is such a thing as *Christian* humanism as opposed to *secular* humanism.

11. True or false: Secularism is the attempt to remove all traces of God from the world.

12. True or false: The student is most likely to be *socially* seduced before he is intellectually or philosophically seduced.

Answers:
1. Yes 2. False 3. True 4. True 5. True 6. True 7. True 8. True 9. True 10. True 11. True 12. True

CHAPTER SEVEN
What About Those Humanists?

In 1948 the Communists took over China and sent the Western world into shock — a shock compounded a year later by Russia's detonation of their first atomic bomb. Congress, at the proding of Senator Joseph McCarthy, launched its witch-hunt for Communists in high places in Hollywood. The church, also determined to do its part, held classes on the deadly peril of atheistic communism. Para-military types were invited to teach Christians the art of surviving atomic attack or Russian invasion.

As a young Christian, I was mystified by it all. I dared to say that I thought the church was more hysterical than thoughtful about what they were saying and doing. This earned me a lot of suspicious looks and some whispers of "pinko," a word in that day for a person who was not a full-fledged red, but a sympathizer.

I feel that I'm going through all this again. Thirty years later, it's not the Communists but the secular humanists who are generating the polemics, though "communist menace" still gets some mileage in the church. I am not saying that Communism and secular humanism are not evil forces to be reckoned with, but I do not believe there is a conspiracy. I would hope that we deal with the issues here more thoughtfully than emotionally or faddishly.

THE FUROR OVER HUMANISM

The January, 1982 issue of *Eternity Magazine* ran several articles on humanism. One of the articles did an excellent job of tracing the battle for and against secular humanism —

a battle that has been going on for several decades.

In 1933 The Humanist Manifesto spelled out the secular side clearly enough, but it was not until the sixties and seventies—when public schools started removing religious habits such as prayer and Bible reading and replacing them with controversial programs—that people started to take notice. The public was further aroused by the 1973 Supreme Court Decision on abortion.

In 1976 the House of Representatives passed an amendment against secular humanism as a religion that was not to be taught in public school. A 1961 Supreme Court decision had already identified secular humanism as a non-theistic religion.

Francis Schaeffer took up the battle with his films "How Should We Then Live?" (1977) and "Whatever Happened To the Human Race?" which later appeared in book form. With C. Everett Koop, the current Surgeon General, he made secular humanism a household word, at least in Christian homes.

Protestants and conservative Catholics took up the battle. One Catholic writer, Joseph Sobran, does feel, however, that the evangelical attack on humanism is losing for two reasons: "One is that they argue poorly. They are unsophisticated and their enemies are very sophisticated indeed.... Secondly, they have been cut off, by their enemies, from their natural allies among other Christians."[1]

The college-bound student needs to understand what the battle is about and how he can fight it. But first he needs to understand what humanism is.

What Is Humanism? The word humanism has been claimed by those who explain human existance without any reference to God. Out of fear of being identified with this philosophy, Christians tend to avoid using this word in any positive sense. But by avoiding it they play into the hands of the secular humanists who would rob us of an important concept in the doctrine of man—that our humanity is actually a reflection of God.

Because the secular humanist gives man the credit for be-

ing able to do too much, the Christian reacts and counters
by going to an unbiblical extreme of making man capable of
doing nothing. I pointed out in the last chapter than man is
capable of doing a great deal. This is his heritage as a
creature made in God's image. We must not attempt to battle the humanists by denying human ability. We must do
battle on the ground that man has a great deal of ability due
to the fact that he is created in God's image. This is one of
the truths Paul articulates in Romans 1 and 2. We must do
battle by making a distinction between *secular* humanism
and *Christian* humanism.

Secular Humanism. The dictionary definition of
humanism is, "A modern, nontheistic, rationalist movement
that holds that man is capable of self-fulfillment, ethical conduct, etc. without recourse to supernaturalism." That's a
good definition of *secular* humanism. Christians should oppose a nontheistic, rationalistic movement that leaves out the
supernatural, but we must not argue that man is incapable
of self-fulfillment or ethical conduct.

Every day we are called on to draw from the resources
we have as human beings. We pursue education and learn
job skills. We learn how to make a marriage work and how
to be good parents. A great deal of self-fulfillment is possible
for us. Many unbelievers are happy, content and fulfilled.
Because they are creatures made in the image of God and
enjoy common grace, they can feel very fulfilled. But
because they are blind to this in unbelief, they assume that
the fulfillment comes by their own doing.

Paul makes it clear that the problem is not man's inability to function as a man. Man, being man, knows God and
is very capable of subduing creation and filling the earth.
But he refuses to give God the glory for this ability or to
thank Him. Man is guilty of the terrible sin of ingratitude.
But he cannot be grateful because he is blind, spiritually. Yet
blindness does not relieve him of his guilt.

The believer differs from the unbeliever in identifying the
source of our human resources. We, as Paul, are in agreement with the Athenians that man is indeed a wonderful

creature. But we hold that man is a marvelous creature because he is made in the image of God—not just any god, but the God of creation, the God and Father of our Lord Jesus Christ, the God of the Bible. It is "in Him we live and move and exist" (Acts 17:28).

The same must be said about ethical decisions. Man is capable of making ethical decisions, not concerning his relationship with God but concerning his relationship with other men. Ethically, he cannot restore himself to God. Only Christ can do that. But ethically he can make some marvelous decisions with respect to this life.

When Air Florida flight 90 crashed into the Potomac at Washington, D.C.'s National Airport, *Time* magazine published an essay called "The Man In the Water." After the crash a man was seen clinging to the tail section of the plane with five other survivors. Each time the rescue helicopter lowered its life-ring, this unknown man, about 50, passed the ring to the other survivors who were lifted to safety. But before he could be saved, he slipped beneath the water. The essay said this:

> "Everything in nature contains all the powers of nature," said Emerson. Exactly. So the man in the water had his own natural powers. He could not make ice storms, or freeze water until it froze the blood. But he could hand life over to a stranger, and that is the power of nature too. The man in the water pitted himself against an implacable, impersonal enemy; he fought it with charity and he held it to a standoff. He was the best we can do.[2]

What were these "natural powers?" Some inscrutable nobility that evolved over billions of years, turning a primeval beast into a god who gives his life for the salvation of others? No, not the evolution of nobility from a beast, but a man created in the image of our Great God and Savior. The seat of those natural powers is in Christ. To deny that such powers exist is to play into the hands of the secular humanist and to deny an important Christian doctrine: the doctrine of man.

It is true that such an ethical decision does not reconcile a man to God. We can never be good or noble enough. Only the perfect nobility of Christ, the King Himself, could possibly satisfy infinite justice. But as far as man's relation to man, we must acknowledge that the unbeliever is capable of marvelous acts because he is made in the image of God.

Christian Humanism. Christian humanism, therefore, seeks to assert the ability of man *as a creature made in God's image*. This is not an ability to rescue himself from his sin. Only God can do that. It is the assertion that man, though fallen, is still declared the image and likeness of God. J.I. Packer says:

> I am a humanist. In truth, I believe it is only a thorough going Christian who can ever have a right to that name....
>
> What is humanism? Essentially, it is a quest: a quest for full realization of the possibilities of our humanity. We see ourselves as less satisfied, less fulfilled, less developed, less fully expressed, than we might be; we have not yet tasted all that could enrich us, nor yet developed all our creative potential, nor yet made the most of relationships with others, nor yet enjoyed all that is there to be enjoyed, nor yet fully harnessed the powers of the physical world as instruments of our freedom; and we long to enter further into what we see as our human heritage. In this basic sense we are all humanists; our natural self-love, which God implanted in us, makes us so. You would have to say of anyone who had ceased to look for personal enrichment in any of these ways (as alas, broken folk sometimes do) that he or she was hereby lapsing from one dimension of humanness, as if to contract out of the human race.[3]

"Contract out of the human race." That's an important statement. As a therapist who deals with troubled people every day, I find that many Christians are suffering for this very reason. They contract out of the human race. They turn their backs on God-given human resources for health and happiness—resources that originate in their humanity, resources that are a legacy of their first birth. They act as though the second birth renders inoperative the first birth. They understand "natural" ability wholly in a spiritual sense, as used in 1 Corinthians 2:14. They make "natural" equal to "sinful." But the word natural is a legitimate description of human nature, which is the image of God. Human nature is the ability to do great and marvelous things because we are the image of God.

In the last chapter I pointed out those scriptures that teach fallen man is still the image of God (Genesis 9:6; 1 Corinthians 11:7; James 3:9). Though man fell spiritually and his relationship with God was severed, he is still man — with all the dignity that word conveys. Metaphysically he did not become less than a man when he fell. Because of that, he is able to exercise marvelous powers of control over himself and this planet, as he was commanded to do (Genesis 1:28). But he will not acknowledge that! Nor will he acknowledge the God who made it all possible (Rom. 1:18-25).

Christian humanism corrects false ideas about Christian doctrine and false philosophies that relate to them. I listed those doctrines and philosophies in the last chapter. They are the sovereignty of God, man the image of God, the fall, common grace, natural revelation, human ability and responsibility, dualism, mysticism and asceticism, humanism, and cultural mandate.

My hope is that Christian humanism will have an impact on the way systematic theology is written in the coming years. Many systematic theologies from the conservative Protestant side tend to make the doctrine of salvation their focal point. By that I mean the other doctrines are presented in such a way as to demonstrate man's need for the saving work of Christ and the subsequent work of the Holy Spirit in sanctification. For example, the fall is presented in such a way as to demonstrate man's utter hopelessness. Indeed, spiritually, he is blind, dead, and lost. But only careful reading makes the inquiring mind wonder, "But in what way is fallen man still the image of God?"

In an otherwise excellent book, Macauley and Barrs in *Being Human* say that the purpose of salvation is to restore the image of God.[4] On the back cover of the book this statement is repeated: "When we are truly spiritual we are

fully human." If that is so, then the Nazis are guiltless for
exterminating the Jews as *subhuman* creatures!

No, a thousand times no! Every Jew that died at Hitler's
hand was a reflection of God's image. The Nuremburg trials
were a vindication of Genesis 9:6. Let no man even dare utter an antisemitic remark. How can we curse men who have
been made in the likeness and image of God (James 2:9)?

I hope that Christian humanism will encourage a more
adequate treatment of the doctrine of man in more
systematic theologies. Man does need to be born again.
Without faith in Christ the Way, he is hopelessly lost and
damned. No good that man ever does will save him (Ephesians 2:8-9). But let us not give Christians the idea that we
have nothing of value in our humanity, and that we turn in
our human-race-membership-cards when we become
Christians—as though we become some sort of other-worldly
creature.

Implications for the Christian Student. It is important
that the Christian student understand the issues involved
here because he will be bombarded by secular humanism
from the day he arrives on campus. Consider, for example,
the following words from leading lights in the world today:

Carl Sagan: "The cosmos is all that is or ever was or ever
will be."

Kurt Vonnegut: "I beg you to believe in the most
ridiculous superstition of all: that humanity is at the center
of the universe, the fulfiller or frustrator of the grandest
dreams of God Almighty. If you can believe that, and make
others believe it, human beings might stop treating each
other like garbage."

Simone de Beauvoir: "At times I wish to finish with life
so as to shorten my anguish. And yet, I hate the annihila-
tion of my existence. I think with melancholy of all the
books read, the places visited, the amassed knowledge: they
will cease to be. The music, the painting, the culture: then
suddenly nothing!" (quotations from Eternity magazine,
January, 1982, pp. 16-18).

You will find these ideas especially pervasive in

philosophy and social science courses. Secular humanism promotes the ideology of welfare liberalism, which seeks to solve human problems through social engineering.

Messianic socialism, particularly as seen in dialectical materialism, is one of the most virulent forms of secular humanism. Dialectical materialism, a philosophy of Marx and Engles, applies Hegel's dialectical method to observable social process. There are no absolute truths, such as the Bible. The idea is that for every thesis there is an antithesis which then yields a synthesis. The Christian student who understands the issues involved in humanism will be able to develop a Christian humanism of his own to counter this teaching on campus.

OTHER "ISMS" TO CONSIDER

There are other philosophies that are also enemies of the faith, and we must guard against them, as well. Each of these philosphies is naturalistic rather than supernaturalistic. Naturalism is an attempt to explain things apart from God.

Because the naturalistic philosophies leave God out, Christians tend to reject important concepts such as *natural* revelation and God's working through *nature* and the *laws of nature*. They also tend to regard man's *natural* ability as sinful. But natural human ability that comes from man's creation in the image of God is not sinful. Human ability and human nature are not the same as the *sin nature* or the *natural man* of 1 Corinthians 2:14. Consequently, we need to be on guard against dveloping an unbiblical view of naturalism. Psalm 19 eloquently proclaims that nature declares the person and work of God day in and day out, night in and night out.

We must also distinguish between the philosophical basis of the error and the issues that the philosophy addresses. Secular humanism is a good example. We cannot agree that man can find ultimate fulfillment or is capable of superior ethical conduct apart from God. But we must not be maneuvered into saying that unbelievers are incapable of good works or ethical conduct. I have already pointed out that unbelievers have a great deal of ability, but not for the reason give by the secular humanist. The unbeliever is able to do a great deal *because* he is made in the image of God.

Christians, falling into the secular humanist's trap, make the mistake of trying to over-emphasize how bad man can be. There's no question that man can be bad, but the secular humanist is correct when he demonstrates that the human race is not as bad as it could be — although he doesn't see that it is because of common grace.

My point is that we must be careful that we are not maneuvered into an indefensible or non-Christian position. Remember: first, *naturalistic* and *natural* are not the same. Naturalistic explains nature apart from God. Natural explains nature with God and sees God's working through it. Second, the philosophies or isms may be false, but they may also touch on issues that the Christian is legitimately concerned with. Let's look at some of these other isms. Fritz Ridenour gives a helpful list of naturalistic philosophies in his book *How To Be A Christian In An UnChristian World.*[5].

Rationalism. This is the idea that man can figure things out for himself. Christians don't deny man's ability to think and be creative. But the Christian sees this ability as a manifestation of man's creation in God's image. The rationalist says man's ability to think and be creative is *apart* from God.

Pragmatism. This is the idea that truth is what works or is that which guides man successfully. Is it useful? Does it bring satisfaction? Christians are interested in things working and being successful in their endeavors, and we know that if things do work, it is because we have discovered how the God of creation makes His creation work. Yet workability is not the final test of truth.

What is more, in approaching pragmatism we need to ask, does it *really* work? What may appear to work may — in the final analysis — not work at all. Take for example a very popular notion introduced in the '60s — that couples can live togehter successfully without the benefit of marriage.

Young people of that era saw marriage as meaningless. They were unwilling to consider what the Bible had to say about it because truth to them was not objectified in the Bible. Truth was what worked. So they experimented — and it was a flop. We have enough historical perspective now to see that "living together" was an emotionally damaging experiment fraught with legal complications.

One young woman I know gave ten years of her life to a relationship that was suddenly terminated by the death of her boyfriend in an auto accident. The insurance settlement went to the young man's parents. Because she had not married, the girl had no legal recourse and was left emotionally and financially bereft.

A large part of my marriage counseling practice involves people in living-together arrangements. They are so emotionally bound together they simply cannot walk away from the arrangement. On one hand they do not choose to marry, or at least one of the partners doesn't so choose. But both seem to feel that to walk away from the relationship would be as emotionally traumatic as a divorce.

What has happened? We were assured in the '60s that we were entering into a brave new era, and the "living together" arrangements would solve the divorce dilemma and all its pain. But it hasn't worked! How many times has the pragmatist placed faith in his experiment only to be hurt?

Utilitarianism. This philosophy holds that truth is what produces the greatest happiness for the greatest number of people. Again, the relativity of this statement creates problems for the Christian.

Denial of the *philosophy* of utilitarianism does not mean that Christians are against the greatest number of people having the greatest happiness, however. Our quarrel is with how it is achieved.

Hedonism. This is the philosophy that unabashedly claims that pleasure is the chief good in life. The words *chief good* are the problem here. We are not against the idea of pleasure, as we often are accused of. What is more, we need to be careful that we don't validate this accusation by going to ascetic extremes and practicing extreme self-denial as a means of attaining greater spirituality.

Idealism. This idea, as developed by the German philosopher George Hegel, teaches that there are no absolutes. There is no longer the true (thesis) vs. the false (antithesis). Hegel's idea is that by bringing the two together, we arrive at a synthesis.

Again the Christian has a problem with this because we must reject the notion that there are no absolutes. Yet we must also be careful that our resistance to the idea doesn't produce a legalism that makes everything black and white.

Evolutionism. This idea uses Darwin's theory of natural selection, that man is the result of millions of years of development from primitive life forms. It implies that man was not created by God in His image and is therefore responsible only to himself and his own standards of behavior.

The Christian must reject this, but he must be careful that he not be maneuvered into presenting an Adam dressed in a Brooks Brothers suit with a Wall Street Journal tucked under his arm. Likewise, we are willing to recognize variety within the classifications of creatures created by God. We must be careful that in denying the philosophy, we are not forced into taking an extreme opposite position that Christianity does not maintain.

Existentialism. This idea holds that life is meaningless and absurd, so man is free to do his own thing as long as he is sincere and is willing to take responsibility for his choices.

Christians reject the idea that life is meaningless and absurd. "Doing your own thing" cannot be accomplished without boundaries that God has set down in Scripture. There is also a place for being sincere and taking responsibility for your choices within these boundaries.

Practically speaking, I don't find that the expressions of this philosophy or any of the other relativistic philosophies really *do* what they claim to do. My own counseling ex-

periences during the '60s and '70s showed me that many
young adults were playing out this philosophy in their
economic and sexual behavior. They refused to go to school
or to work or to develop job skills. That was *their* business,
they maintained. They also insisted their free and easy sex
life was also their business, and they were hurting no one.
This kind of irresponsibility produced thousands who
now are unable to be productive members of society and
have become an economic burden, complaining that the
government won't take care of them. Similarly, the sexual
behavior that was "hurting no one" produced hundreds of
thousands of illegitimate babies whom the state was left to
care for, as well as an epidemic of VD that is costing us
billions in health care. Where does accepting responsibility
for one's choices begin, then?

Nationalism. Nationalism elevates the values and traditions of the nation over the autonomous individual (as in
classical liberalism) or the political party (as in communism).
Nationalism, though it poses as the family's defender, really
subordinates the family to national interest.

The danger comes from both the right and the left. The
policies of Nazi Germany with its Hitler Youth Movement
had the same goal as Communist Russia has with its Communist Youth Movement. It's interesting that American fun-
damentalism is able to see the danger from the left but is
myopic on the right side.

I view with alarm much of the family legislation that is
going on in government today. Certainly, legislation is needed to redress the grievances of women in the work force
who are struggling as single parents and are not receiving
court-mandated child support from their ex-husbands. Certainly children need to be protected against abusive parents.
But we must be careful that we do not set precidents that
will enable government to subordinate the family to national
interest.

Technological Materialism. This world and life-view sees
utility, efficiency and productivity as prime virtues. The ag-
ed, retarded and severely handicapped who make no "con-

tribution" have no place in this system. The technological materialist encourages the dependence of humanity on technology. To him, technology and productivity are our salvation.

The mood of the college student today is quite different from what it was in the '60s and '70s, and it reflects some of this technology-materialism. Students today are more serious about study and have a great deal of concern about getting a good job. Now with the nation in the throes of economic change, I believe this life-view will gain greater popularity.

Nihilism. This is the denial of all norms and values. It is fostered by the technological mentality, which elevates efficiency over ideology and religion. Social institutions and norms that stand in the way must be pushed aside. Bloesch calls the nihilists "the new barbarians, who are intent on destroying rather than creating, but they destroy in vain hope that something new and durable will result."[6]

International terrorism is one manifestation of nihilism. Likewise, nihilism is at the core of Japanese industrial might. Connected with a form of nationalism, it tends to make the individual and family part of the larger family, the corporation, which is the favored child of the State. Americans, who have long admired the Japanese system, are attempting to import it. We run some great risks in mindlessly applying the system, however.

These "isms," then, are foes to be reckoned with. But in doing so, let's fight back with a Christian humanism that elevates man as created in God's image. Man is unable to work himself back into fellowship with God because he is saved by grace not works (Eph. 2:8-9), but he *is* capable of marvelous achievements on earth.

One ism I have not yet mentioned, because I want to treat it in some detail, is mysticism. I want to focus on it because I believe that it is subverting more Christians than any other false philosophy.

REVIEW CHAPTER 7

1. What is secular humanism?
2. What is Christian humanism?
3. Is natural ability sinful?
4. True or false: When a person becomes a Christian he becomes fully human.
5. Match the letters and numbers of the two lists below. For example, the philosophy (1) Rationalism goes with (D) the idea that man can figure out things without god.

1. Rationalism	(A) the truth is whatever works.
2. Pragmatism	(B) the values and traditions of the nation are more important than the individual.
3. Utilitarianism	(C) pleasure is the chief good in life.
4. Hedonism	(D) the idea that man can figure out things without God.
5. Idealism	(E) utility, efficiency and productivity are valued above all else.
6. Evolutionism	(F) there are no absolutes like good and bad.
7. Existentialism	(G) truth is whatever produces the greatest happiness for the greatest number.
8. Nationalism	(H) life is meaningless, so do your own thing.
9. Technological Materialism	(I) denies all norms and values.
10. Nihlism	(J) man was not created in God's image but evolved from a lower type of life.

CHAPTER EIGHT
Beware Of The Mystics

Oh how the thought of God attracts
And draws the heart from earth,
And sickens it of passing shows
And dissipating mirth!

'Tis not enough to save our souls
To shun the eternal fires;
The thought of God will rouse the heart
To more sublime desires.

God only is the creature's home,
Though rough and straight the road;
Yet nothing less can satisfy
The love that longs for God.

Frederick William Farber (1814-1863)

These three stanzas from the hymn "The Way of Perfection" voice a sentiment that at first reading may appear Biblical and noble. What is more, the Christian and Missionary Alliance luminary A.W. Tozer included this hymn in *The Christian Book of Mystical Verse.*[1]

Yet the hymn reflects a sentiment that is positively unbiblical! The idea that the earth and all that is in it is "sickening" and "dissipating" when compared to God Himself is a mystical sentiment based on ancient Greek error. So also is the concept that the "shows" and "mirth" of this earth are to be shunned for the "more sublime desires" that are found above in God, who "only is the creature's home."

WHAT IS MYSTICISM?

Tozer declares mysticism a "personal experience" with God. He says that the mystic differs from the ordinary orthodox Christian only because he experiences his faith down in the depths of his sentiment being while the other does not. He exists in a world of spiritual reality. He is quietly, deeply, and sometimes almost ecstatically aware of the Presence of God in his own nature and in the world around him.[2]

Tozer seems to be saying that the Christian mystic is just more experience-oriented in his faith than is the "ordinary" Christian. Yet some of the verse he includes in his book reflects far more than that. It sounds similar to the sentiment found in the ancient modern heresies of the church.

> Am I not enough, Mine own? enough,
>   Mine own, for thee?
> Hath the world its palace towers,
> Garden glades of magic flowers,
>   Where thou fain wouldst be?
>
> Fair things and false are there,
> False things but fair.
> All shalt thou find at last,
>   Only in Me.
>
> Am I not enough, Mine own? I, for ever
> and alone, I, needing thee?
>
>   *Gerhard Tersteegen (1697-1769)*[3]

How can the God who declared His creation good now say in this verse that the palace towers and garden glades of magic flowers are *false?* How can a God who said, "It is not good for man to be alone" say in this verse, "Am I not enough?" *No,* He is not! God made mankind social beings *with a need for each other,* not just for Himself alone.

If by mysticism Tozer means religious enthusiasm, then that is quite proper. But historical mysticism has been at the root of many heresies because it tries to bypass the intellect and an understanding of scripture in its quest for God. It also has a strong ascetic element. It denies pleasure and power in its quest for union with God. It usually is a world-denying philosophy. By "world" I don't mean the anti-God system the Bible speaks of. It is world-denying in that it sets up an antithesis between the spiritual (and heavenly) — which

is seen as good—and the material (and earthly)—which is
seen as evil.

The secular humanist celebrates the fulfillment of the self,
whereas the mystic emphasizes the loss of self in God. This
is what makes mysticism particularly dangerous for the
young Christian today. It offers the Christian what appears
to be an answer to the secular humanist's glorification of
man. The mystic loses himself in God. What is more, the
mystic sounds biblical to the untrained ear.

What we hear today is exactly what we heard from the
mystics in the early church. Take for example Saint
Palladius of the Church at Alexandria, who said, "All those
who love Christ make haste to be joined to God through
these virtuous acts, each day preparing for the release of the
soul."[4]

Acts of asceticism, the denial of the body, were encouraged by the ancient mystics to hasten the release of the
soul from the sinful body. Isidore, the elder of the Church
of Alexandria, until the end of his life wore no fine linen except for a headband and neither bathed nor ate meat—all
evidences of denying the flesh. Commenting on the common
ascetic practice of not bathing, Rushdoony wryly comments
that it tells us something about what the ancients meant by
"the odor of sanctity."

THOSE TROUBLESOME GREEKS

Flight From Humanity. The Greeks under Plato's influence maintained that God, who is spiritual and holy,
could have nothing to do with that which is material and
evil. This is known as "dualism." In the early history of the
church the heretics, following this idea, went so far as to
deny that Jesus had a human body. It was unthinkable that
the invisible God should reveal Himself in human form.
They explained away the body of Jesus as just a phantom.
This is why 1 John 1 goes into detail about the Jesus who
could not only be seen and heard but handled as well. John
was making the point that Jesus was a real human being. He

was no phantom. He was indeed God in the flesh.

Neoplatonism, a school of philosophy that developed from this early Greek thinking, emphasized that ideas were more important than substance. Therefore, the superior man would ignore the material world in favor of the mind or spirit.

Clement of Alexandria sanctified this pagan idea and introduced it into the church. He held that the truly devout would therefore renounce the material for the sake of the spiritual. It wasn't long before the human body was viewed as a prison-house of flesh that held captive the truly spiritual soul. The liberation of the soul from that person was to be achieved by despising material things, denying the fleshly body and concentrating on spiritual things. The exercise of prayer became, as a result, less a medium of guidance and more a means of escape from the material world.

This is not far from ideas current today. The idea of being lost with God in meditation or rapturous prayer seems like a legitimate exercise to many Christians. On the surface it looks fine — and it is fine if it merely is an expression of love. But too often it becomes an escape from the realities of life.

Man Without Feeling. To the Greeks and many in the early church the ideal man was detached from the material world. He was man without feeling, as far as this world is concerned. He was not troubled by feelings — or if he was, he could lay the blame on a lustful body in which his pure spirit was imprisoned — a prison from which he sought release.

We see this expressed in a passion for ideas rather than people. The *person* is ignored. The result is a lot of intellectual gush, and in religious circles, pious gush — the *idea* that we ought to be closer to God while really failing to love in a practical way those who are around us. Rushdoony gives an example of this in a prayer he heard once in a prayer meeting:

Lord, be merciful unto me, poor sinner that I am. I sometimes go
a whole hour doing my work and never thinking about you.
How can I, who have known such sweet joys in your presence,
fall into such sin as to forget you for a whole hour. My heart
breaks with the knowledge of my failure to love you as I should.
Possess my soul with a never-ending passion for you, that I may
every moment be near to the heart of Jesus and be filled with the
sweet passions of your grace and love, etc., etc., ad nauseam.[5]

Rushdoony says in comment,

"This woman was negligent of her ordinary responsibilities as a
daughter, wife and mother. Her refuge from responsibility was in
pious gush and sanctimonious peity. The purpose of her prayers
was to impress on others her closeness to God and to make them
feel ashamed that they, unlike her, were not going around their
work in religious ecstasy day after day. She was without faith or
works; she had replaced both with pious gush."[6]

Michael Wigglesworth. This dualistic heresy continued
through the period of the Middle Ages of the church and on
into the later era of the Puritans in the 17th century.
Though the Puritans generally had a healthy outlook on the
human body and all of its functions, including sex, a notable
Puritan poet, Michael Wigglesworth, popularized the ancient
error, and was largely responsible for the popular notion
that the Puritans were sexually repressed people.
    His heretical thinking is most evident in his Diary written
while he taught at Yale. Rushdoony captures the essence of
Wigglesworth's mystical error. He says:

Like a good neoplatonist, Wigglesworth found his body a sore
burden and a real embarrassment. He was deeply distressed by
the fact that he farted; this made his "life a burden," and, amaz-
ingly, moved him "To carnal lusts." The fact was that any
reminder that he had a body had a distressing effect on Wigglesworth, but, like all would-be ascetics, the more he tried to
forget his body, the more vocal his body became. Wigglesworth
regarded the flesh's needs with horror: "witness my daily sensual
glutting my heart with creature comforts." The expression
"*creature* comforts" is especially revealing; the neoplatonist is not
willing to be a creature. Certainly Wigglesworth *never* rejoiced in
being a creature; instead he seemed to mourn with no small
caterwauling, that he was not pure spirit.[7]

Sex was a vile problem to him, and noctural dreams and emissions were a horror. He wrote, "I loath myself, and could even take vengeance of my self for these abominations."[8] And though it may seem strange in this "sexually enlightened" age, I recall counseling a devout, young college boy who was obsessed with the idea of castration to rid himself of fantasies of the opposite sex. He sincerely believed that such would be a spiritual act, but he just couldn't bring himself to do it — further evidence to him of "the weakness of the flesh" and his inability to "live the Godly life."

MODERN MANIFESTATIONS OF UNBIBLICAL MYSTICISM

The student who would avoid the pitfalls of mysticism in the classroom and on the campus must be aware of some modern manifestations of this ancient heresy.

Other Labels. A common way the heresy is dispensed in the classroom is by relabeling. Sometimes the relabeling is very subtle. For example, "prayer" and "meditation" as practiced by Far Eastern religions is said to be equivalent to Christian prayer. The serene and simple manner of the devotees are held up as an example of the peace these people achieve in their religion.

The comparison is not valid. The peace found in the religions of the Far East is psychological rather than theological. I'm not knocking psychological techniques as a way of achieving tranquility. But when a religious system is built out of it and declared to be on par with Christianity, that's another matter. The peace the Christian receives is theological. That is, once an enemy of God because of sin, he is now reconciled through faith in Jesus Christ and His sacrificial death. This may also bring a secondary benefit of *psychological* peace. To be at peace with God should yeild good feelings. But those feelings are based on a reality that other religions cannot have without Christ.

Double Meanings. Another way this heresy is dispensed, particularly in Christian circles and among Christian friends,

is in spiritual formulas and words that carry two meanings.
Let me list them and comment.

1. *"Trusting God"* and *"Letting go and letting God."* A big
calculus exam is coming up and Bert is very anxious. If he
fails, he'll flunk the course. Bert can't eat or sleep, and one
of his friends tells him that he's not trusting God. Is this
true?

Maybe yes; maybe no. If Bert properly understands the
doctrine of human ability and responsibility and has diligent-
ly applied himself to his studies, then maybe he isn't trusting
God. Of course a wise counselor will inquire carefully about
Bert's study habits and lifestyle. If Bert has applied himself
and has studied, "trusting God" is in order. If God wants
him in that school or in that course of study, then he can
rest confidently on a successful outcome. If God wants him
elsewhere or in a different course of study, He may use this
as the occasion to move Bert.

If on the other hand Bert refuses the discipline of study,
it is sheer presumption to "trust God" or "let go and let
God." Such is not faith but mental gymnastics.

A variation of thesis "waiting on God." Again, human
responsibility often is ignored. However, if Bert has studied
and has taken the exam, "waiting on God" is appropriate. He
has done all he can. He can do nothing else. This waiting is
not an oriental serenity exercise. It is objective faith in the
sovereignty of God. Nor is waiting a cop-out of his responsibility to study. It comes after Bert has studied. This is *our*
part and *God's* part.

2. *"The devotional life"* and *"having devotions."* Jamie is
having trouble with her parents. Every time she talks to
them on the phone or visits them, they have a terrible fight.
Finally, they threaten to cut off financial support. Jamie is in
a constant state of anger, which often overflows in conversa-
tions with her friends. One of her friends suggests that her
problem is her devotional life—she doesn't pray or read her
Bible enough. If she were having her devotions as she ought,
she wouldn't be so angry and she'd find the peace she seeks.

Is that so? Maybe yes; maybe no. If Jamie is not seeking

God's guidance about what she should do, then yes. Among other things, God uses Scripture and prayer to guide. If, on the other hand, prayer and Bible reading are being advocated to elevate her above the troubles of the world and to lose herself in communion with God, then she is behaving like the Hindu who finds psychological release by becoming oblivious to the problem of the world through religious exercise.

3. *"Praying through."* Jamie also might be told by others that she ought to "pray through." Is that the answer? Maybe yes; maybe no. If the idea of urgent prayer is being advanced in praying through, then, yes. The judge heard the widow's urgent plea in Jesus' parable.

If on the other hand prayer is seen as an exhausting labor that is regarded as meritorious work, then, no. It was the widow's *attitude* of urgency, not her hard work that was rewarded.

4. *"We can do nothing."* Jamie might also be told by her friends that her problem is that self has not been broken. The spirit cannot work because the outward man must be broken and she must realize that she can do nothing. Galatians 2:20 is often quoted in support of this notion.

Galatians 2:20 does not mean that the self is replaced by the Spirit. Paul's "I" continues to live. He lives by the power of the Son of God. He does not live autonomously.

Ephesians 5:18 tells us not to be drunk with wine but be filled (under control) with the Spirit. Just as wine needs a *person* to make drunk and control, so also the Holy Spirit needs a person to control. He does not replace the person.

5. *"The world and the flesh."* The enemies of the spiritual life are declared by the Bible to be the world, the flesh and the devil. The world is the system of ideas and ideals that are opposed to God. The flesh is the sin nature.

We must be careful, however, that we don't confuse the world as used above with the world as God's physical creation which was declared good in Genesis 1 — a goodness reaffirmed in Acts 10:15. Christians often act as though disengaging from God's creation is spiritually meritorious.

Yet the voice commands, "Arise. Kill and eat! What God has cleansed is not unholy."

The word "flesh" is also confused. The Bible uses the word in two senses. In the ethical sense, the flesh is our sin nature. But in the metaphysical scene, the flesh is our physical body. We are encouraged to meet the needs of the physical body. This is good health. Yet mystics, in the interest of subduing the sin nature, deny the physical body thinking that somehow that will subdue the sin nature. That is not biblical.

Darlene was a very lonely young lady. She was home from school for the summer and had trouble being separated from her boyfriend. She missed him. A well-meaning aunt told her that she was being troubled by the flesh and ought to pray for victory. She was to pray that Christ would take the place of this fleshly need.

The aunt created two problems. First, she was hinting that this human need was somehow sinful. Darlene's desire to be with her boyfriend was evidence of being troubled by the flesh. Human need was equated with sinfulness.

Second, the aunt was suggesting that this human need could be replaced by Christ. The aunt was unaware that God had said it was not good for man to be alone. The aunt would agree with the hymn, "Am I Not Enough?"

6. *"Human nature."* The Bible talks of a sin nature, but it is often confused with human nature. Human nature is the expression of our humanity as created in the image of God. Human nature is what Jesus took on with His Divine nature to become the God-man. Human nature, therefore, is not sinful. Otherwise Jesus Christ would have taken on Himself a sin nature.

Human nature is a perfectly legitimate aspect of the Christian who functions in the image of God. What rises from our human nature is not to be cursed as sinful but rather blessed as a reflection of Him who made us.

Roberta's Letter. Several years ago a woman suffering severe depression sent a mimeographed letter to her friends to let them know that she had gained the victory over her depression. For some reason I was on her mailing list.

She was a battered wife. As with many battered wives, I think she also was a very self-effacing person. She opened her letter by saying she discovered that depression is caused by our not being close enough to the Lord. Her solution was to get closer: "I found I could get so close to the Lord that I had no physical or mental pain. It was nothing of my own doing because I prayed all the time."

Roberta was practicing mysticism. She found "release" from her pain by fleeing this earth and getting closer to God. Prayer and Bible study were not used as a means of guidance out of her situation, but as an escape from it. Prayer for her was much like an Eastern mantra. She used it to take her mind off her trouble.

After telling of her beating at her husband's hands she said, "The next morning I arose, prayed sincerely, studied my Bible as sincerely as ever, and prayerfully studied and learned.... I am going to let the Holy Spirit work in me all day and night. But then the power doesn't work in me unless I pray and study and pray and study about it most all the time..."

Notice she believes that prayer and Bible study are what "brings the power." She is not talking about God's guidance through His Spirit and His Word, but of escape—of becoming oblivious to her problems. The idea that the power comes through hard work—the work of prayer and Bible study—is similar to the heathen idea that God shall hear us for our much speaking.

Note also her desire for God to "engulf" her. Again, the mystical idea surfaces. We are engulfed or lost in God in a rapturous experience produced by the work of Bible study and prayer. It is there that she found she had no pain.

I don't doubt that she had achieved painlessness and composure, but it was not through Biblical Christianity. She had achieved it by psychological means, just as a mystic from the Far East might. She simply used Christian labels and cliches.

Summary. The Christian student on the secular campus is

going to be bombarded by a naturalistic approach to life that denies supernaturalism. This approach will deny that God is the author, sustainer and finisher of His creation. The student must be on guard against this.

But I believe that the student faces a greater danger. It is the danger of mysticism. And he may fall into this danger as a reaction to naturalism. We must not permit the naturalist to force us into a position of denying sound Biblical doctrine because we don't want to sound naturalistic. Creation and God's working in His creation rightly belong to the Christian. Human nature rightly belongs to the Christian. We are made in God's image and likeness. Let us therefore treasure the legacy of our first birth as dearly as we do the legacy of our second birth.

REVIEW OF CHAPTER 8

1. True or false: The mystic attempts to escape the physical world and his body in order to achieve complete union with God.

2. True or false: Mysticism is dangerous because it denies the worth of our humanity.

3. True or false: Human nature is evil and therefore ought to be eradicated.

4. True or false: When you experience the second birth (are born again), you no longer have need of anything from your first birth, your humanity.

ANSWERS:
1. True
2. True
3. False
4. False

CHAPTER NINE
The Moral Jungle

"I worked in the Greek systems at both Auburn and the University of Alabama at Tuscaloosa. The attitude in many of the sororities was, 'If you are going to be involved physically with someone, you'd better be discreet about it!' A couple of girls weren't, and they were kicked out. They had to sit the term out.

"Here at Maryland sexual involvement is a status thing. Two girls I work with have roommates who let their boyfriends sleep with them all night. They'll even have sexual relations while the roommate is still in the room! My friends have to find another room to sleep in!"

Phares Wood, senior woman Crusade staffer at the University of Maryland, has found that the moral climate in colleges today differs from campus to campus. "At Maryland, guys can be in the dorms 24 hours a day. When you have that kind of rule, you're going to have sexual promiscuity. At Alabama the only time guys could be upstairs in the sororities was from one to six on Sunday afternoon."

Rusty Stevens agrees with Phares that the moral climate is not the same on all secular campuses. Rusty is the Navigator representative at the United States Naval Academy in Annapolis. A graduate of the academy himself, Rusty spent six years in the nuclear Navy before returning to the academy with the Navigators.

"A service academy is more committed to traditional values than many state schools are. You have the honor concept, for example. Midshipmen don't lie, cheat or steal. But a lot of immorality still exists. They are not as open about it; they have to be careful, too. It used to be that if you had a history of VD you couldn't get into the academy."

I asked Rusty if the middies get much chance to chase women and booze it up. He said, "The men get a significant amount of liberty, so they're not cooped up. And booze is part of the military life. You know the image — hard fighting and hard drinking."

What Rusty was saying sounded a lot like the attitude at Alabama. On some campuses discretion is as important as academic performance. But there is a sense in which the campus with high moral values may be more dangerous to some Christians. I asked Rusty how a Christian would be influenced compromise his faith in a service academy where alcohol, drugs and sexual promiscuity are covert. He said, "There's a danger of giving up living for Christ and living for yourself — becoming selfish and imitating what appears to be popular. For example, foul language, a haughty and prideful attitude and running over other people to get ahead."

A CAMPUS SURVEY

As I listened to Phares and Rusty I wondered if the attitudes they reported were fairly typical across the country. I wondered, how legitimate is the concern of Christian high school students, parents, pastors and youth workers over the moral big three: booze, drugs and premarital sex? Is it just a local phenomenon?

I decided to spot-check some campus workers around the country to see what they could tell me. My information comes from people who have had personal contact with students on nine major campuses in the United States.

Randy Butler is on the Intervarsity Christian Fellowship (IVCF) staff at the University of Southern California in Los Angeles. The student population at USC is about 25,000. I asked Randy to tell me about the moral "big three" at USC.

"There's a lot of pressure on the incoming freshman to rush and pledge a fraternity or sorority. It's the socially dominant system here, although only a minority — about

2,000—embrace it. Fraternity and sorority life has its own pressures not so much drugs, but drinking and sex. Those who are not involved in the Greek system—those in dorms and other student housing—also feel the pressure. I don't hear a lot about drugs right now, except for some pot and coke, but there's a lot of drinking—especially beer."

The pressures at William and Mary, in Williamsburg, Virginia, are more academic than social, according to Frank Venable, IVCF campus staffer. A smaller school with only about 5,500 total student population, William and Mary isn't a "party school," Frank explained.

"The partying social scene is pretty much limited to smaller groups on campus, although there are dorm parties and that sort of thing. William and Mary is very academic, almost to the point of being academically oppressive.

"A freshman coming in is used to being number one in his high school class, but he's going to face a big challenge with the academic pressure. Those who are not able to remain at the top of their class look for social alternatives— drinking, minimal use of drugs, and of course sex. It's not all over the place, but it's there if they want it.

"You'd probably have to go to a place like Wheaton to avoid open booze and sex," Frank continued. "I want to point out that we're talking about two very different schools. William and Mary is a secular college where you face real-world life, issues and happenings on campus. At Wheaton the environment is pretty much protected. That's nothing against Wheaton—it's an excellent school. I realize I'm biased, in that I'm a minister to the secular college campus."

I wanted to know what the homosexual scene looked like at William and Mary. Frank said, "About two years ago a homosexual group established itself on campus. Lambda Chi is the name of it. They were given the rights of a student group, so I suppose they have a charter and everything. It's died down a little bit, but it's definitely there. That might suggest something of the climate here.

"I graduated from the University of North Carolina at Chapel Hill, and there was much more of an active, visible group there. I graduated in '78, so my information is a bit dated. College campuses change rapidly. Carolina is like UVA. It's a party school. The partying and the drugs, at least in '78, were quite a problem there. Pot was fairly prevalent in the dorms and fraternities."

The University of Texas has a student population of about 40,000. Pete Wilson is an IVCF Campus Staffer there. He had some helpful things to say about the moral tone at UT.

"I've been trying to figure out what some of the newer problems are here, new developments. The thing that pops into my mind is that this year there seems to be more sexual activity in the dorms — one-night stands. A lot of the students go to parties expecting to find someone who will go with them — have some kind of relationship with them. Sexual activity used to be mostly living together relationships, but now it seems to be more the one-night stand thing. In some dorms you don't have it at all, but in other dorms it's taken for granted.

"As far as alcohol, last week [April '82] there was an article in the campus newspaper about the increase of alcohol-related accidents on the campus — car accidents and other problems. They said there was a definite increase in drinking on campus.

"As far as drugs are concerned, Austin is a notorious drug center. There is quite an overlap between students and town people drawn to the campus. There's a lot of drug news around here, but how much is strictly university, I can't tell. There's a lot of marijuana use.

"I graduated from Duke in 1972, and the big three were ever-present. There were people who were regularly cohabiting, and the one-night stand was not so much in evidence then. I can remember coming in as a freshman and seeing almost no marijuana in the dorms, but within a year or two you could smell a lot of it around. It really came into the school from high school kids who had picked it up during the years 1968 through 1970.

"I do feel that booze, drugs and premarital sex are

legitimate concerns, but it would vary from dorm to dorm according to what kind of social life you found. Some dorms are large and there's not too much interaction; you might form two or three friendships and be left alone. In smaller dorms there is more social pressure and interaction, so I would say it's a hit or miss thing right now. Some kids will feel a lot of pressure, and other will be able to pull through without much pressure.

"Most of the schools set up an older brother type of program, someone to squire you around campus during your first days there. I found this even at Duke. When I was there it was assumed that these guys would take you out drinking to places in town right off the bat. That's about the only thing that should be considered. If incoming students are paired off with upper classmen, they're liable to wind up under pressure to drink. They should get in touch with a Christian campus group so they can avoid getting into the big brother thing. They should get to know Christian upper classmen right away."

What about the homosexual scene at UT?

Pete answered, "They're pretty quiet, but they're well established. More was going on a few years ago, but they now have a center for themselves on 'The Drag', which is the main area of stores and shops right next to the campus. It's very prominent. They're like a lot of groups who make a lot of noise at first until they get organized. Then they settle down. Right now they're pretty quiet, but here in Austin the gay lifestyle is more tolerated than in other places. They feel pretty much at ease here. You might see lesbians walking around holding hands, but don't see the exhibition of it by guys.

"One other thing, in terms of moral climate. Parents send their kids to schools that are reputed to be Christian, but sometimes these schools are not really too conservative. Baylor's religion department teaches the higher critical approach to Scripture, for example; and Trinity University in San Antonio — a Presbyterian school — is, in my opinion, also quite liberal."

One reason the moral climate on campus might indicate serious problems with sex, alcohol, and drugs is that the faculty may be endorsing such behavior by default. Without consciously realizing it, the members of the faculty become teachers of morality.

TEACHERS OF MORALS

The attitude of adults toward morality teaches youth far more than anything they can put into words. These attitudes are taught through the rules, or lack of them. When an administration says it's okay for a guy to be in a girl's room 24 hours a day, they're saying it's a matter of no concern to them what goes on between a man and a woman in a campus dorm. Some will defend their stand — or lack of it — saying, "It's not our job to enforce a moral code." Yet such disclaimers don't represent the situation as it really is. The administration and the faculty are not morally neutral. Again and again they betray a permissive bias, both by the lack of rules on the campus and by the things they say and do in the classroom.

Lani Stephens, Rusty's wife, is a graduate of the University of Maryland. She articulated this clearly. "I remember a health class in my freshman year — that was 1972. We were discussing alcohol and drugs, and a teaching assistant asked if anyone there actually abstained from alcohol. The way the question was phrased and the tone in his voice made it obvious that anyone who raised his hand would look stupid. The way he talked encouraged ridicule of anyone who raised his hand. You would have to have some strong convictions to raise your hand. It was a big class — about 200 — in a curved theatre where everyone could see you."

Other students tell me that ridicule and intimidation in the classroom are common. Freshmen students are easily intimated because they are anxious to fit into the system.

Lani shared another example that said something about the school's attitude toward alcohol.

"I was a biology major, and one day one of my pro-

fessors came to class drunk and with a bad case of the
shakes. He didn't teach many undergraduate courses—mostly
upper level. But it was commonly known that he was an
alcoholic. Everybody joked about it.

"It's hard to believe I was paying good money for
something like this. I remember a lot of times sitting in my
classes thinking, if these kids' parents knew what they were
paying for, they would be shocked—up in arms! Even if
their parents weren't Christians, they wouldn't respect a lot
of these people, and certainly they wouldn't want them in-
fluencing their children. All my professors weren't that way,
but I saw quite a few sad cases in my four years."

SEX ON THE SECULAR CAMPUS

Usually when you hear talk about sex on the secular
campus, you think of men and women sleeping around. And
often the attitude is, "I'll be okay if I stay away from that."
But there's a little more that you ought to know about.

Lani Stephens and Sue, Rhonda, and Marti (three
Maryland coeds whom I've mentioned before) shared some
interesting experiences about sexual problems on campus. I
asked them what the incoming freshman can expect.

Lani shared more of her classroom experiences. "We were
studying the British writers of the 1800s, and all the professor could talk about was the sexual symbolism and in-
nuendo in their writings. It's okay to understand those
things, but the whole course seemed to revolve around
discovering those innuendos.

"Another professor I had," Lani continued, "also looked
for the hidden sexual references, and whenever he found
one, he would laugh! My impression was that he thought
the students found it funny, too.

"I saw girls—who had come in as eager and innocent
freshmen—graduate with a cynical, hardened attitude. It
wasn't just their classroom experience, though. They were
getting involved sexually. But the attitude in the classroom
certainly reinforced those destructive decisions."

"Even in the school newspaper," Rhonda added, "you'll see people advertising for mates—gay or straight. You're going to be exposed to it in writings, in obscenities, and even sexual harrassment."

"It's sometimes difficult to walk across campus without being harassed," Marti commented. "My roommate had an eight o'clock class, and one morning she went to the copy machine at the undergraduate library before class. Some guy exposed himself to her—at eight o'clock in the morning!"

"That happened to one of my friends, too," Sue added. "She's been to the police station twice to identify the guy in a lineup. The same guy keeps exposing himself to her!"

"A friend of mine was jogging," Rhonda put in, "and some guy was doing weird things behind the stairs. Then he followed her. She decided against running behind the stairs again, and she went another way—and there he was again! What was she supposed to do? It happens."

Much of the time the problem isn't men who are exposing themselves or bent on rape, but men who are on the prowl. Marti's advice to the Christian girl coming on campus is never to bring a guy into your dorm or dorm room, never to let him know your name or where you live.

"Sometimes it's so innocent, the way they ask," Marti explained. "They'll say, 'So, where do you live? Are you new on campus? Do you live in Somerset?' Don't be naive, be cautious."

"A friend of mine was studying in the library one day," Rhoda added. "A guy at another table had been staring at her for about three hours. He had a book, but he kept staring at her. She felt uncomfortable, so she decided to take a break, walk over to another building, and get some hot chocolate. He followed her, introduced himself, and asked her where she was going.

"She told him that she didn't care if he walked with her, but that she was dating someone special. That night she got a phone call from him. She had make the mistake of giving him her name. One thing that's bad on campus is that the student directory lists your name, address, and phone number. That's how he got her phone number."

"That brings up something else," Sue interjected. "Don't put your name on your books! I've seen more girls get in trouble because their names were plastered all over their books."[1]

"What are you supposed to say when they ask your name?" Marti asked. "You don't want to be rude. We're so scared to be rude that we set ourselves up—and we forget they are being rude to us!"

If you smile and look embarrassed or as if you don't know what to do, you've giving a submissive message. But if you give a verbal and non-verbal message like, "Hey, what's the big rush? I don't give my name out," you're saying to him, "How dare you!" Let him know you're no pushover. More often than not a guy will back off. Sometimes he'll try to one-up you by ridiculing you and calling you uppity, but don't crumble, and don't smile.

Christian girls are still being taught to be ladylike and courteous, and a smile means submission. A guy is going to take that smile as an invitation, like,, "Ah, ha! She's interested!" It's hard because we usually try to relieve tense social situations with a smile that says everything's okay.

"But," someone may ask, "how does being rude and icy square with Jesus' command to be light and salt?" Sue feels that it's a matter of being wise as serpents and harmless as doves. A girl needs to think of safety first. She's not going to be much of a witness as a corpse in a parking lot.

This does not mean that Christian girls should be paranoid. But they should practice safety first. There are plenty of opportunities to be light and salt in situations that are not dangerous. But even under those circumstances, where it's not a matter of danger but of a socially sticky situation, a Christian girl doesn't want to act like a pushover.

Girls aren't the only victims of sexual harrassment, however. And guys aren't the only ones on the make. The girls are just as bad. Dave, whom I mentioned earlier in the book, told of his experience on campus.

"It all started the first night I was on campus. A girl tried to pick me up. Thank God I didn't know what to do! But it sure opened my eyes to see how available they are. The first party in the dorm, *four* girls tried to pick me up," Dave explained. "Freshmen girls just like to go wild. Freshmen guys—all guys—pick up on that. Girls have become a big moral issue for me and for other guys, too. They're so *available*."

"That's an understatement," Sue interjected. "But you do have two types. Some stay very straight, like I did. Others don't. In my freshman year it was a common thing for the girls to get smashed. I remember walking into the bathroom one morning and hearing deep snoring coming from one of the stalls. I thought, *Oh my gosh, there's a guy in there!* I went running out. Several of us tiptoed in, opened the door, and we couldn't believe it. There was a girl in there, out cold, with her skirt over her head!

"We even had to tie one girl in her bed one night because she was so smashed she was trying to drink bleach. But the pressure to drink and to have a guy was for status—like, how many guys did *you* get? I spent the night with a friend on campus and got the shock of my life to see girls coming in really smashed during the weekend. I don't know how much of a problem it is in other dorms, but it sure was at the college I attended."

"With all the crowd around, it might seem difficult to 'get it on' with somebody," Dave added. "But the guys will either go back to the fraternity house or to the dorm or take the girl to a hotel.

"Yet a lot of guys eventually grow up. They seem to calm down. There may be some regrets, but not a whole lot. They still have the same drives, but it's not the juvenile 'keeping score' kind of thing that it once was—how many beers and how many girls. They will still go out, but sex becomes a more private thing."

THE HOMOSEXUALITY SITUATION

The classified ad in the campus paper under "Services"

reads, ADAM AND ED GAY MALE DATING CLUB. The
phone numbered offers 24-hour information. It's not
uncommon.

On one campus the gay element may be quite active. On
another, less visible. But the gay community can also create
a great deal of sexual pressure on the unwary student. I
asked Sue and Dave to tell me what their experiences have
been.

"At Maryland they're quite active," Dave explained.
"They're really coming out. This semester they have a Gay
Awareness Week. Each day something happens—a gay
barbeque, a gay beer party, and a gay support day where
everyone who supports the gay will wear blue jeans.
Everybody on campus wears blue jeans anyway! No one has
propositioned me, but I see a lot of literature and stuff."

"At a college I attended, it was horrendous," Sue said.
"Very high incidence, including the hall where I lived. My
roommate and I spent a lot of time with one girl who really
was upset and was thinking of caving in to the lesbian
pressure there.

"I shared Christ with another girl, and she became a
Christian. But there were some in the physical education
department who were really after her. She got involved in a
horrible situation. That was a big problem at school."

What guidance can be given to concerned parents or high
school seniors to avoid problems when they come on to a
campus? Sue says the biggest factor is friends.

"Get involved with Christian kids who have their act
together," she urges. "Get into activities that get you away
from the pressures. Watch the way you dress. Be careful
regarding the physical education thing, and if you feel like
you're in trouble, get professional help.

"Keep in close contact with your parents. I've noticed
that the girls who get into homosexual relationships succumb
to pressure from people who offer them affection. Their lesbian friends accept them just the way they are, and when
they do get involved, their straight friends find out. Then
they are branded as lesbians, shut out of the straight world

and locked into the lesbian world."

Sue and Dave and everyone else I talked to about suc-
ceeding on the secular campus as a Christian kept coming
back to the same thing—friendships. Who you spend your
free time with is all-important in the development or destruc-
tion of your character.

SEX ISN'T FUN ANYMORE

My work puts me in touch with the intimate details of
people's lives. Over the past couple of years I've become
aware that the younger set isn't as excited as it used to be
over sexual liberation from moral strictures. I thought it was
because of the psychological and physical punishment
resulting from sexual promiscuity. I figured young people
had begun to discover that free love isn't so free.

Then one day I walked past an airport newsstand and
saw on the cover of *Rolling Stone* magazine, "Why Sex Isn't
Fun Anymore." I couldn't believe it! *Rolling Stone*, of all
magazines! I had to read it. The story was called "Lovesick:
the Terrible Curse of Herpes." In bold print, the subtitle emphasized, "Twenty million Americans have it and will for the
rest of their lives."

This well-written and well-documented story was about
the current epidemic of the herpes simplex virus (HSV) Type
2. Closely related to Type 1, the common cold sore, Type 2
infects the human genitalia, buttocks, thighs and stomach
and hides between outbreaks. Some people are constantly
debilitated by it. Others suffer from recurrent outbreaks.
Lymph glands swell and are tender. Muscles ache and the
victim is feverish. A rash appears, develops into pox-like
blisters, which later become ulcerated running sores and then
scabs.

Not only is herpes physically debilitating, sex usually is
painful. Pantyhose or jocky shorts may no longer be
tolerated because of the sensitivity of the genital area.

The popularity of oral sex has given rise to an interesting
twist. Doctors are now finding Type 2 around the mouth

and Type 1 in the genitals.

The typical herpes sufferer becomes infected at age 18. By age 33 he is settled down with a family, but debilitated by a chronic disease with a reputation that adds to the suffering. "These are young, active people who have never been sick before," said San Francisco physician Richard Hamilton. "They don't know *how* to be sick. When I open the door to examine someone who has herpes, it's usually like walking into a wall of goo. As a group they're defensive, guilt ridden, and angry at the medical profession—some of them are *severely* depressed.... There's a lot of 'why me?'"[2]

The herpes epidemic, estimated to be on the increase at a rate of 500,000 to a million cases a year, is only part of the story. Between October 1980 and 1981, over a million cases of gonorrhea were reported. The fastest growing VD is NGU, a form of gonorrhea, estimated to be infecting 2.5 million people a year.

Chastity was suggested as a solution in a companion story, but *Rolling Stone* thought the idea was "downright demoralizing." Demoralizing or not, there is a practical reason for behaving yourself. It's called VD.

BACCHUS AND MARY JANE

It's no news that Bacchus and Mary Jane are alive and well on the college campus. It appears, however, that alcohol is growing in popularity over drugs. One reason is that it's legal and readily available.

The most popular drink on campus is beer. As of 1978 28 states permitted 18-year-olds to buy and drink beer. But even in the states that set the drinking age at 19 or 21, the 18-year-old is not deterred. His social set includes people of 18 to 22 or older. All you need is someone with a valid ID to buy a case for a party.

Almost all college social events revolve around beer, and sometimes spiked punch. Alcohol is used to "lubricate" the party to loosen inhibitions. There's also a certain status that goes along with how many beers you can put away and still navigate. I talked with Dave, Sue, Marti, and Rhoda about it.

Sue noted that friendship is often first offered at beer parties. "Here's the first opportunity to get to know people and get a chance to fit in. Beer lowers inhibitions, and you become instant buddies."

"If you're worried about being accepted," Rhoda added, "it seems like the thing to do. If you don't, you just don't fit in with the rest of the crowd. If you want to be like the gang, you'll drink. You're hit with it the first night on campus."

Speaking of drugs, Dave said, "There are still plenty of them. Quaaludes [a sedative called methaqualone]. I've never done drugs, but they're definitely available. Beer is driving it out because it's not illegal and it's more available. Hard liquor isn't as much of a problem, except maybe for spiked punch. Mostly guys are interested in how much damage they can do to a case of beer—how much can you put away. A guy's considered great if he can put down two sixes and not feel it."

"I remember going to my first beer party," Sue added. "It was at someone's house. I was with a guy I knew from class, and I didn't want him to get in bad shape. All evening I would take his beer and pour it through the slats in the gazebo we were in. I whispered to him, 'They'll never know, even though they're keeping count.' He thought it was funny. We'd switch glasses, and I'd pour it through the slats. His buddies were really impressed with how much he was putting away. He hardly had any.

"We talked the next day and I said to him, 'Didn't you have fun not being drunk last night?' He said, 'Yeah. Actually, I did.' But the funny thing is that everything was okay so long as everyone else *thought* he was drinking a lot. That was the whole thing. He didn't really care about getting drunk. But it was the status thing—how many beers he could put away."

I asked about marijuana—is pot a status thing, too?

"Not too many people do that stuff," said Dave. "It's

more among the guys who did it in high school. A lot of guys use speed when they're studying for exams and finals. But even that's not too common. No status goes along with it, because pot is more private than social."

"But I smell marijuana in my hall all the time," Marti interjected. "It depends on the people you hang around with. I don't hang around with non-Christians that much, so I don't hear much about it. When I was living in Elkton, and I wasn't walking with the Lord, I heard about drugs all the time. I was hanging around with people who used drugs. Marijuana — and cocaine — were very prevalent. But coke's expensive, so you don't get as much."

I asked what happens if the RA [Resident Advisor] smells marijuana on the hall.

"They're probably in there doing it with them," Marti replied. "The RAs really aren't very responsible. They're not police kind of people. They're more like the person who wants to set up the pot party. They have to interact with everyone on the hall and they have to keep peace in the dorm, so they want to be known as good guys. They're not about to report anybody for drug violations. So you'll have in the dorm some coke, pot, and some acid — but not much. More uppers and stuff to keep you awake for studying.

"We also have Christmas Trees," Sue added, "especially during exam week. That's some kind of upper [dexamyl] to keep you awake.

"On our campus," Rhoda said, "there's mainly pot and people doing Rush to get a high real quick. Rush is fumes that rush to your head. It gives you a high, maybe for fifteen to twenty minutes."

"A lot of that kind of stuff only lasts two minutes at most," Marti put in. "I've seen people do it. They get this little bottle and sniff. It's really stupid because they usually get a bad headache from it. There are a lot of bad side affects, too. It can damage internal organs — especially the liver and the brain." Abusing sex, drugs or alcohol can create problems for the rest of your life.

ACADEMIC DISHONESTY

There is another moral issue apart from the big three that the Christian needs to consider. It is the matter of academic dishonesty.

The student needs to know that any act of academic dishonesty presents the danger of suspension or expulsion from college. The student also runs the risk of having future educational or employment opportunities jeopardized. In accordance with federal regulations disciplinary records for dishonest are open to prospective employers and educational institutions.

Academic dishonesty includes the following:

1. Cheating — intentionally using or attempting to use unauthorized materials, information or study aids in any academic exercise.

2. Fabrication — intentional and unauthorized falsification or invention of any information or citation in an academic exercise.

3. Facilitating academic dishonesty — intentionally or knowingly helping or attempting to help another to commit an act of academic dishonesty.

4. Plagiarism — intentionally or knowingly representing the words or ideas of another as one's own in any academic exercise.[3]

Whether it is a matter of dishonesty or of sex, drugs, and alcohol, there is good reason for you to be concerned and aware of the moral environment of any campus you select. Whether you attend a school with a reputation for partying or for strong traditions or for heavy academic pressure, you will have to make some decisions about these kinds of temptations. That is why your relationships are so vital to you.

Earlier I pointed out that the seduction of the mind does not begin with an attack on your ideas. It begins with relationships. When we find a person who is attractive to us, we begin to enjoy that relationship and lifestyle. Only then do we begin to consider the philosophical justification for behavior patterns. We begin to doubt our own philosophy because it gets in the way of what we want to do, and the social education of our minds has begun.

Dr. Frank Peters, past president of Wilfred Laurier University in Kitchener, Ontario, carries this one step further, particularly as it relates to morals. He says that when young people say they have an intellectual problem with their faith, they are probably having a moral problem in reality. The moral problem comes before the intellectual problem. The real intellectual problem is that what they believe runs contrary to how they're behaving. Rather than get rid of the immoral behavior, they try to jettison their faith. Dr. Peters goes to far as to say that *who* you hang around with is more important than *what* you believe!

REVIEW OF CHAPTER 9

1. True or false: You can expect to find the temptations of alcohol, drugs and premarital sex on all college campuses.

2. True or false: A professor's attitude toward morality teaches us as much as anything he can say.

3. True or false: There's nothing wrong with a girl's giving a male stranger her name, phone number or address.

4. True or false: Girls experience peer pressure to drink and get involved sexually just like guys.

5. True or false: Herpes Simplex Virus (HSV) Type 2 is curable.

6. True or false: Talk of a "VD epidemic" is just scare talk to keep college kids from having sexual relations.

6. False
5. False
4. True
3. False
2. True
1. True
ANSWERS

CHAPTER TEN
Countdown To College

The average high school senior simply doesn't know that he's unprepared for college. He's somewhat awed by the complexities of it all, and more than anything else he hopes he will fit into the system with a minimum of embarrassment, but as with most things, he's confident he can muddle through! This is the nature of high school seniors. Perhaps you are different, but either way, it is time for you to take on more responsibility for yourself. It is a step toward adult maturity.

Nonetheless, you are going to need the support of your parents, and so the bulk of this chapter is addressed to them. After you have read it, ask them to read it, too. Then discuss with them some of the questions this chapter raises, and begin to work together toward establishing yourself in college.

Your part. Do you want college badly enough to spend the necessary time and mental energy it's going to take to get in? If you are not willing to do this, perhaps you are not ready for college. The discipline of getting into college is really a good test of your interest and readiness. Consider the following questions:

1. Are you willing to take the time to sit down with your parents and discuss college — why you want to go, what you want to get out of it, and where you want to go? I'm not talking about a single discussion. I'm talking about frequent discussions that occupy your family's time during the closing months of your junior year in high school, all summer, and the opening months of your senior year.

Giving yourself time to think and talk about college is important because most teenagers tend not to think ahead. All of your life your parents have done it for you. Now you have to take this responsibility and become aware that you just can't muddle through; you'll lose out if you try.

2. Are you willing to take time and spend the necessary mental energy to do some interest testing if necessary to sharpen your focus on college? It's no crime for you to be unaware, but you will never be a good student if you are unwilling to become aware. That's what college is all about.

3. Are you willing to put a percentage of your money into the college effort? This may mean carrying some of your fees or some of your own support. This is important because students who get a free ride often do not take their education seriously. If you are making some contribution to your own support, it's unlikely that you will waste this opportunity.

This may mean a summer job or a part-time job during the school year. You should talk with your parents about what they expect these earnings to go toward. This should not be discretionary income for you to use as you please. Your parents probably have little discressionary income of their own. Why should they have to tighten their belts and not expect you to do the same? This is part of your education in adult reality.

4. Are you willing to take the time and to exert the mental energy to gather necessary documents such as SAT scores and high school transcript? Are you willing to apply yourself to the drudgery of filling out, with your parents' help, the application for admission?

Your parents may find it easier to do it themselves, but remind them that it won't help you learn responsibility or understand the admissions process. It also continues the illusion that your parents will do whatever is necessary to get you into college and keep you there. This doesn't make for a very responsible college student.

For Parents Only. The attitude of you, the parents, is very important. You must be patient, but you should not do

your son's or daughter's work. You may need to prod your
student gently to take the necessary steps to get into college
and be willing to let your student miss his chance to get into
college if he balks.

Sometimes parents want college for the student more
than he wants it for himself. This leads to ugly scenes and
confrontation. *The student must want college for himself,*
and want it badly enough to apply himself to the admissions
procedure. If he doesn't, he will not succeed in college no
matter how helpful you are. You can't take college for him.
The time has come when he has to want something badly
enough that he's willing to work for it — or fail.

"We found a lot of interest on the part of the adults, but
the high school kids really weren't that interested." This was
the comment of Ray Cotton, Administrative Services Director of Probe Ministries, an organization that conducts "College Prep Seminars" for churches that want to prepare their
high school seniors for the secular college campus. The
seminar covers philosophical issues such as creation-science
and the nature of man. It also offers practical help in better
study habits and how to live a balanced Christian life on a
secular campus. Each of the students receives a college prep
notebook in the seminar.

Because of lack of student interest, Probe isn't pushing
this seminar too vigorously. Instead, they offer another
seminar for students already on campus called, "The Christian World-View Seminar." They have found that once the
student is confronted by the issues on campus they're more
interested. "The high school student is on the top of the
world," says Ray. "You find yourself telling him he has problems he doesn't know he has yet. He's not interested in
that. So, we're putting more emphasis on the seminars for
the college kids."[1]

By the time most young people reach the age of 18, they
are almost deaf to their parents' voices. It is a natural part
of growing up. Often, they even lack interest in what seems
(to the adult) to be the most important factors of preparation for their future.

So it seems that the only way an 18-year-old learns is by making his own mistakes. Do you love your uncooperative child enough to let him fail—and learn thereby?

Let me give you an example. Suppose you let him know when his deadline is for application for admission. You have reminded him of the documentation he needs to send with it, but your efforts to get him to cooperate with you in getting this done meet with repeated indifference or even ugliness. Are you willing to patiently let him miss the deadline for application?

Or, let's say that he does get into school and that it's agreed that he will have a summer job to pay for his clothes, automobile expenses (insurance and gas) and have spending money. But he puts off getting a job or is too picky about the kind of work he'll do. Are you willing to let him face the opening of the term with no money for the above obligations and patiently shrug your shoulders and tell him it's not your problem?

Parents who are too helpful can be as much a problem as parents who are not helpful enough. If the student is to accept his academic responsibilities, he must demonstrate that he is a responsible person.

ISSUES TO REVIEW

You can help your high school student by reading each chapter of this book and discussing the review questions at the end of each chapter together. The purpose of the review is to provoke discussion and help the student understand the important issues of each chapter. They should not be treated as an exam, however. Don't make it a grim affair. If the student doesn't understand the chapter or the review questions, explain them.

What College Is And How It Works. The student should be aware of the fact that college is designed to help him think clearly and not to teach him job skills. He should be aware of alternatives to a four-year college, such as junior college with a transfer program or alternative programs like correspondence and proficiency exam.

He should know the difference between undergraduate and graduate schools. He should know where professional schools fit into the scheme of things, and he should have an acquaintance with the titles and functions of campus administrators such as chancellor, provost, and dean of students.

Which College To Go To. You should discuss with the student his choice of college. What are realistic options for him? Much depends on geographical location, cost, program and the ability to gain admission.

Discuss with the student his interests and go over the college choice check list on pages 39-40 if he has the option of attending several different colleges. You may also want to have him take some interest tests such as those described on page 38. These may help him make a little more intelligent choice of school.

Though there may be some risk in not being able to transfer credits, remember that if the student finds that a different college would suit his needs better after his first or second year, he can be open to the idea of a transfer.

Financing College. Discuss with your son or daughter where the money is coming from to finance the education well in advance of high school graduation. Make it clear to the student what you expect of him in terms of helping to pay for his education as well as his housing and maintenance.

If financing college is a serious problem, the student may have to resort to alternative ways of earning credit. Students who have been taken care of all their lives may take it for granted that their parents will do the same through four years of college. You cannot expect the student to be realistic about his expectations of you unless you discuss the matter with him. If the student does need to resort to alternative ways of earning credit, you will have to help him through the maze of options.

The student who has been dependent on the parent for 18 years is not prepared to take care of many practical matters discussed in this book. You will have to take the lead in helping sort through what appears to be a mammoth task to your teenager. I suspect that some students become discouraged about going to college because of the seemingly impossible hurdles in getting there. He must be very motivated, and your help will encourage him.

Housing Alternatives. All the housing alternatives should be discussed. If the student intends to live at home and commute to college, it is particularly important that he has a clear understanding of house rules and what is expected of him while he lives at home. The student must not think that he can have the lifestyle of an independent adult while living with you. The fact of the matter is, neither he *nor* you are independent adults as long as you live together. Common courtesy demands we give up some of our independence when we choose to live with someone else.

Campus Contacts. Visit the college your son or daughter is planning to attend and get a feel for the atmosphere and the physical layout. Introductions to Christian campus workers and Christian upperclassmen ought to be made at this time. They should be encouraged to contact the student and cultivate him because freshmen are sometimes timid or negligent about making Christian contacts. Often they just develop friendships with whomever they happen to meet, which is not a good way to get started.

Understanding the Unsaved. Your child should have an appreciation for the unsaved on campus, however. Unbelievers are not lying in wait to seduce him, he should remember that the people he hangs around with will determine the character of his social life, which will influence how he thinks, for good or for bad.

The unbeliever should be valued as a creature made in God's image. The Christian student should live and witness with the prayer that he or she may be used of God to help non-Christian students come to faith in Christ.

The student would do well to be aware of the different non-Christian philosophies so he can recognize them when he hears them. He should be aware that the basic philosophical difference the Christian has with the unbeliever is that the Christian sees God as the author, sustainer and finisher of His creation. The unbeliever sees man as functioning without need for any god or at least for the God of the Bible. The Christian is a supernaturalist and the unbeliever is a naturalist.

Christian Groups. The student should be guided carefully in the selection of Christian fellowship. I see a grave danger in the student's being drawn into a fellowship that looks and sounds very spiritual but in reality is steeped in mystical error. Too often Chistians react to the naturalistic philosphies on campus by going to the other extreme — unbiblical supernaturalism as expressed in mysticism and a Christianity that is almost totally experience oriented.

Moral Issue. As a parent do not suppose that lecturing or moralizing on the evils of booze, drugs, premarital sex, or academic dishonesty will help your son or daughter. By now he knows where you stand. His greatest protection against falling into these temptations will be a socially rewarding Christian fellowship. In an atmosphere of social fulfillment the Christian has the best chance of strengthening his moral convictions.

Understanding the college scene — both in terms of its mechanics and the Christian concerns on the secular campus — is difficult enough for the educated adult. For the high school student, it is a maze of mystery. Everything he needs to know about college is overwhelming. To supplement the information I have provided for you here, you will want to examine the appendix of this book. You may also need to refer to the list of abbreviations and the glossary when you correspond with the colleges that interest you and your young adult.

Just going through the discipline of getting into college will be a major step toward maturity for the college-bound high school student. As his parent, you will be tested for your ability to be supportive and patient; but when the struggle is over, you will see that it has provided your young person an excellent opportunity for growth.

APPENDIX A

GLOSSARY

Definitions of commonly used terms vary from college to college. Consult specific college catalogs for more detailed information.

Accreditation. Recognition by an accrediting organization or agency that a college meets certain acceptable standards in its education programs, services, and facilities. Regional accreditation applies to a college as a whole and not to any particular programs or courses of study. Specialized accreditation of specific types of schools or professional programs is usually determined by a national organization, such as American Association of Bible Colleges, American Chemical Society, etc. Regionally accredited colleges are identified in their *Handbook* descriptions. Information about specialized accreditations is given in *Accredited Institutions of Postsecondary Education.*

Achievement Tests (ACH). College Board tests in specific secondary school subjects, given at test centers in the United States and other countries on specified dates throughout the year. Used by colleges not only in deciding about admissions but also in course placement and exemption of enrolled freshmen.

Admissions Testing Program (ATP). A program f the College Board that provides college entrance tests and services for students planning to go to college. Included are the Scholastic Aptitude Test, Test of Standard Written English, Achievement Tests, and the Student Descriptive Questionnaire.

Advanced placement. Admission or assignment f a freshman to an advanced course in a certain subject on the basis of evidence that the student has already completed e equivalent of the college's freshman course in that subject.

Advanced Placement Program (APP). A service of the College Board that provides high schools with course descriptions in college subjects and Advanced Placement Examinations in those subjects. High schools administer the examinations to qualified students, who may then be eligible for advanced placement, college credit, or both, on the basis of satisfactory grades.

American College Testing Program Assessment (ACT). Test battery of the American College Testing Program, given at test centers in the United

States and other countries on specified dates through the year. It includes tests in English usage, mathematics usage, social studies reading, and natural sciences reading. The composite score referred to in the descriptions of some colleges is the average of a student's scores on these four tests.

Appellate Board. A judicial panel that hears appeals from other disciplinary boards.

Assistant professor. A teacher one rank above instructor. He may hold a masters degree or higher.

Associate Degree. Degree, such as Associate in Arts (A.A.) or Sciences (A.S.), offered by a two-year college.

Associate professor. A teacher holding next-to-the-highest rank. Usually must have a doctoral degree.

Audit. Taking a course for the information gained rather than for credit. Usually, fees are charged for auditing courses.

Bachelors Degree. Degree such as Bachelor of Arts (B.A.) or of Science (B.S.) offered by a four-year college.

Basic Education Opportunity Program (BEOG). See Pell (Basic) Grant Program.

Bursar. Cashier.

Business Officer. Person responsible for the financial management of the school.

Calendar. The system by which an institution divides its year into shorter periods for instruction and awarding credit. The most common calendars are those based on semesters, trimesters, and quarters.

Candidates Reply Date Agreement (CRDA). A college subscribing to this agreement will not require any applicants offered admission as freshmen to notify the college of their decision to attend (or accept an offer of financial aid) before May 1 of the year the applicant applies. The purpose of the agreement is to give the applicants time to hear from all the colleges to which they have applied before having to make a commitment to any one of them.

Chancellor. Top administrative officer of a multiuniversity system. Answers to the Board of Trustees or Regents.

College Board. A nonprofit membership organization which provides tests and other educational services for students, schools and colleges. Membership is composed of more than 2,500 colleges, school systems and education associations. Representatives of the members serve on the Board of Trustees and advisory councils and committees that consider the programs of the College Board and participate in determining its policies and activities.

College-Level Examination Program (CLEP). A program of examinations in undergraduate college subjects and courses that provides students and other adults with an opportunity to show college-level achievement for which they have not previously received credit. The examinations are used by colleges to evaluate the status of adult applicants who have not attended college (or not done so recently), students transferring from other colleges, and entering freshmen. They are also used by business, industry, government, and professional groups to satisfy education requirements for advancement, licensing, admission to further training, and other purposes.

College preparatory subjects. A term used to describe admissions requirements or recommendations. It is usually understood to mean subjects from the fields of English, history, social studies, foreign languages, mathematics, and science.

College Scholarship Service (CSS). A service of the College Board that assists postsecondary institutions, the federal government, state scholarship programs, and other organizations in the equitable distribution of student financial aid funds. By measuring a family's financial strength and analyzing its ability to contribute to college costs, CSS offers a standardized method of determining a student's need.

College Work-Study Program (CWSP/CW-S). A federally sponsored program that provides jobs for students with demonstrated financial need. Generally, students are paid at least the federal minimum wage (pending legislation may permit subminimum wages in certain circumstances), and the jobs are available through colleges as well as public and private nonprofit agencies.

Community College. A two-year college, often called junior college.

Comparative Guidance and Placement Program (CGP). A system of information gathering and interpretation designed by the College Board to help students in self-evaluation and in academic and career planning, to assist educators in the placement and counseling of those students, and to provide institutions with summary data for planning and research purposes.

Conference Board. A judicial panel dealing with complex or contested student disciplinary cases.

Counseling Center. Assists students with personal problems and career planning.

Consortium. A voluntary association of two or more colleges providing joint services and academic programs to students enrolled in member institutions. Typical consortiums are made up of neighboring colleges. Students at one campus are allowed to attend courses and use the facilities at other member campuses.

Cooperative education. A college program in which a student alternates between periods of full-time study and full-time employment in a related field. Students are paid for their work at the prevailing rate. Typically, five years are required to complete a bachelor's degree under the cooperative plan, but graduates have the advantage of having completed about a year's practical work experience in addition to their studies. Some colleges refer to this sort of program as work-study, but it should not be confused with the federally-sponsored College Work-Study Program.

Dean. Administrative assistant to the president, in charge of all activities of the college.

Dean of Students. Person responsible for the well-being of students on campus.

Deferred admission. The practice of permitting students to postpone enrollment for one year after acceptance to the college.

Descriptive Tests of Language and Mathematics Skills (DTLS/DTMS). A
set of nine diagnostic and placement tests used by colleges for entry-
level placement and by students for self-assessment of strengths and
weaknesses in important language and mathematics skills. The tests are
offered by the College Board to assist students in self-directed learning
activities and to help colleges in providing appropriate instruction.

Director of Admissions. Person who determines the eligibility of students
seeking admission to college.

Disciplinary Probation. A sanction imposed for violation of disciplinary
regulations. The student shall not represent the college or university in
any extracurricular activity or run for or hold office in any student
group or organization. Additional restrictions or conditions may also
be imposed. Notification will be sent to appropriate college or university offices, including the Office of Campus Activities.

Disciplinary Reprimand. A sanction imposed for violation of disciplinary
regulations. The student is warned that further misconduct may result
in more severe disciplinary action.

Double major. Any program of study in which a student completes the requirements of two majors concurrently.

Dual enrollment. The practice of some colleges of allowing high school
seniors to enroll in certain courses while completing their senior year.
These students are not considered full-time college students.

Equal Education and Opportunity Officer (EEEO). Responsible for im-
plementing the Human Relations Code.

Early admission. The practice of some colleges of admitting certain
students who have not completed high school — usually students of ex-
ceptional ability who have completed their junior year. These students
are enrolled full time in college.

Early decision. Early decision plans are offered applicants who are sure of
the college they want to attend and are likely to be accepted by that
college. An early decision application is initiated by the student, who is
then notified of the college's decision earlier than usual — generally by
December 15 of the senior year.

Early Decision Plan (EDP-F, EDP-S). Colleges that subscribe to this plan,
which is sponsored by the College Board, agree to follow a common
schedule for early decision applicants. Colleges may offer either a
single-choice plan (EDP-S) or a first-choice plan (EDP-F). A student applying under a first-choice plan must withdraw applications from all
other colleges as soon as he or she is notified of acceptance by the
first-choice college. A student applying under a single-choice plan may
not apply to any colleges other than his or her first choice unless re-
jected by that institution. If a college follows the College Board Early
Decision Plan, applications (including financial aid applications) must
be received by a specified date no later than November 15, and the college agrees to notify the applicant by a specified date no later than
December 15.

Expulsion (Expell). A sanction imposed for violation of disciplinary regulations. The student is permanently separated from the college or university. Notification appears on the student's transcript. The student also

will be barred from the campus. Expulsion usually requires administrative review by the school's top administrative officer.

Extension Programs. Educational programs at the college level for those unable to attend the full-time college day program.

Family Financial Statement (FFS). A financial information collection document of the American College Testing Program's Financial Aid Services, used by parents of dependent students or independent students to supply information about their income, assets, expenses, and liabilities. The ACT Program uses this information in estimating how much money a family is able to contribute to a student's college expenses. Can be used to apply for a Pell Grant (Basic Grant).

Federal Institutions, Undergraduate. Service academies such as West Point, Naval Academy, Air Force Academy, Coast Guard Academy and Merchant Marine Academy.

Financial Aid Form (FAF). A financial information collection document of the College Scholarship Service used by parents of dependent students or independent students to supply information about their income, assets, expenses and liabilities. The CSS uses this information in estimating how much money a family is able to contribute to a student's college expenses. Can be used to apply for a Pell Grant (Basic Grant).

Foreign Student Information Clearinghouse. Provides information to foreign students who are interested in studying at the undergraduate or graduate level in the United States. Developed by the National Liaison Committee on Foreign Student Admissions in cooperation with the Directorate for Educational and Cultural Affairs of the International Communication Agency, the Clearinghouse uses information provided by colleges in a computer system that matches specifications provided by students. Students receive a list of selected institutions that best meet their individual requirements, including preliminary information about admissions criteria, on-campus services for foreign students, educational costs, and housing.

4-1-4. A variation on the semester calendar system, the 4-1-4 calendar consists of two terms of about 16 weeks each, separated by a one-month intersession used for intensive short courses, independent study, off-campus work, or other types of instruction.

GED. See Tests of General Educational Development.

Grade-point average or ratio. A system used by many colleges for evaluating the overall scholastic performance of students. It is found by first determining the number of grade points a student has earned in each course completed and then dividing the sum of all grade points by the number of hours of course or carried. Grade points are found by multiplying the number of hours given for a course by the student's grade in the course. The most common system of numerical values for grades is $A=4$, $B=3$, $C=2$, $D=1$, and E or $F=0$. Also called quality-point average or ratio.

Graduate School. Educational level above the undergraduate, four-year college.

Grant. Student aid (gift) usually given where need is demonstrated.

Guaranteed Student Loan Program (GSL). A federal program that lets students borrow money for educational expenses directly from banks and other lending institutions (sometimes the colleges themselves). For the current rate, see the U.S. Department of Education booklet called "Five Federal Financial Aid Programs." You may receive a copy by calling toll free 800-638-6700. The federal government pays the interest while the student is in college. Repayment terms are favorable, and repayment need not begin until completion of the student's education.

Higher education. Education above the high school level, including universities, four-year colleges, separately organized professional schools, and junior colleges.

Honors program. Any special program for very able students which offers the opportunity for educational enrichment, independent study, acceleration, or some combination of these.

Independent study. An arrangement that allows students to complete some of their college program by studying independently instead of attending scheduled classes and completing group assignments. Typically, students plan programs of study in consultation with a faculty adviser or committee, to whom they may report periodically and submit a final report for evaluation.

Instructor. Lowest rank of teacher in a college, usually holds a master's degree.

Intensive Educational Development program (IED). Provides comprehensive and continuous academic advising and tutoring for the physically handicapped and others who are unable to meet the standard student regimen.

Interim Suspension. Suspension for a period of time while disciplinary proceedings are being considered or the student is undergoing medical evaluation. Such suspension usually does not require prior notice, particularly when the student is a substantial threat to himself or others.

Internships. Short-term, supervised work experiences, usually related to a student's major field, for which the student earns academic credit. The work can be full or part time, on or off campus, paid or unpaid. Student teaching and apprenticeships are examples of internships.

Judicial Panels. Boards or committees established under the Code of Student Conduct, designed to conduct hearings on violations of the Code of Student Conduct.

Junior college. A two-year college, often called a community college.

Master of Arts. Degree offered by a graduate school.

National Direct Student Loan Program (NDSL). A federally funded program that provides loans for the undergraduate student. For the current rate, see the U.S. Department of Education booklet, *Five Federal Financial Aid Programs.* To secure a copy call toll free 800-638-7000. Repayment need not begin until completion of the student's education. Repayment terms are favorable, and repayment may be partially or wholly waived for certain kinds of employment.

Need analysis form. A financial information collection document used by parents of dependent students to supply information about their income, assets, expenses, and liabilities. Independent students file these forms for themselves. The information is then used to estimate how much money a family or student is able to contribute to a student's college expenses. In many cases a single need analysis form is the only document that students need to submit to be considered for all types of institutional, state, and federal financial aid.

Open admissions. The college admissions policy of admitting high school graduates and other adults generally without regard to conventional academic qualifications, such as high school subjects, high school grades, and admissions tests scores. Virtually all applicants with high school diplomas or their equivalent are accepted.

Pass-fail grading system. Some colleges permit rating students' quality of performance in their courses as either passing or failing instead of giving grades to indicate various levels of passing work. The college's entire grading system may follow this pattern, or it may be an optional one for individual students in specific courses.

Parents Confidential Statement (PCS). The Parents' Confidential Statement to the College Scholarship Service, which assists in determining financial aid. This form is available from your college financial aid office.

Pell (Basic) Grant Program. A federally sponsored and administered program that provides grants based on need to undergraduate students. Congress annually sets the dollar range. A Pell Grant cannot exceed ·$2,100 per year, but Congress can set a lower ceiling. Students apply directly to the federal government. The FAF or FFS can be used to apply for a Pell Grant. Formerly this was known as the Basic Educational Opportunity Grant Program (BEOG). The pamphlet *Five Federal Financial Aid Program* carries current information on this. It can be secured by calling toll free 800-638-7000.

Pennsylvania High Education Assistance Agency. Provides the PHEAA form that may be used to apply for a Pell (Basic) Grant.

Post-secondary education. College.

Preadmission summer program. A special program in which a student attends college during the summer preceeding the freshman year. The program may consist of remedial studies to strengthen preparation for freshman courses, one or more of the regular freshman courses to enable the student to carry a light schedule in the freshman year, or both.

Preliminary Scholastic Aptitude Test/National Merit Scholarship Qualifying Test (PSAT/NMSQT). A shorter version of the College Board's Scholastic Aptitude Test administered by high schools each year in October. The PSAT/NMSQT aids high schools in the early guidance of students planning for college and serves at the qualifying test for scholarships awarded by the National Merit Scholarship Corporation.

President. Top administrative officer of a college or university. Answers to the Board of Trustees or Regents.

Professional School. An educational institution, which is usually part of a university, that trains students with bachelor degrees in the fields of technology, medicine and theology.

Professor. Teacher of the highest rank, usually required to hold a doctoral degree.

Provost. Academic vice-president responsible for all educational activities. Answers to the president.

Quarter. An academic calendar period of about 11 weeks. Four quarters make up an academic year, but at colleges using the quarter system, students make normal academic progress by attending three quarters each year. In some colleges, students can accelerate their programs by attending all four quarters in one or more years.

Regents, Board of. Board of Directors of a state college or university.

Registrar. Person in charge of official student records.

Reserve Officers' Training Corps (ROTC). Programs conducted by certain colleges in cooperation with the United States Air Force, Army, and Navy. Local recruiting offices of the services themselves can supply detailed information about these programs, as can participating colleges.

Restitution. A sanction imposed for violation of disciplinary regulations. The student is required to make payment to the college or university or to other persons, groups, or organizations for damages incurred as a result of violating the Code of Student Conduct.

Rolling admissions. An admissions procedure by which the college considers each student's application as soon as all the required credentials, such as school record and test scores, have been received. The college usually notifies applicants of its decision without delay.

Sanctions. An official action dealing with violation of the Code of Student Conduct, such as expulsion, suspension, disciplinary probation, disciplinary reprimand or restitution.

Scholarship. Student aid (gift) given for merit, and sometimes, financial need. Examples would be an academic scholarship for students with a high GPA or athletic scholarship for gifted athletes. To qualify for an athletic scholarship a student usually must meet minimal academic requirements.

Scholastic Aptitude Test (SAT). The College Board's test of verbal and mathematical reasoning abilities, given on specified dates throughout the year at test centers in the United States and other countries. It includes the Test of Standard Written English whose questions evaluate the ability to recognize standard written English, the language of most textbooks. Required of substantially all applicants by many colleges and sponsors of financial aid programs.

Secondary education. High school.

Semester. A period of about 17 or 18 weeks which makes up half of the usual academic year in colleges using this kind of calendar. See also Calendar, 4-1-4, Quarter, and Trimester.

Senate Committee on Student Conduct. A judicial panel that hears appeals on expulsion or suspension.

Student Advisors. Assists students with class schedules, and offers information on required courses and eligibility for different programs.

Student Aid Application for California (SAAC). A form used to apply for a Basic (Pell) Grant.

Student Descriptive Questionnaire (SDQ). A questionnaire that can be completed by students when they register for the Scholastic Aptitude

Test or Achievement Tests. It gives the student an opportunity to provide information about educational objectives, extracurricular activities, self-perceived skills, and areas in which counseling or assistance may be needed. The responses are sent, along with test scores, to each student's high school and designated colleges and scholarship sponsors. For those students who give their permission, the SDQ is also used by the Student Search Service.

Student-designed major. An academic program that allows a student to construct a major field of study not formally offered by the college. Often nontraditional and interdisciplinary in nature, the major is developed by the student with the approval of a designated college officer or committee.

Student Eligibility Report (SER). This report qualifies the student for a Basic (Pell) Grant. It is sent four to six weeks after application for the grant.

Student Search Service. A College Board program designed to help colleges identify potential applicants with the particular academic or personal characteristics they are seeking. The service also provides students with an opportunity to learn about colleges with programs and characteristics they want. Information is gathered about students who wish to participate through the Student Descriptive Questionnaire of the ATP and the biographical section of the PSAT/NMSQT. The College Board then supplies each participating college with the names and addresses of students who have the particular characteristics they specify. The service is free to students.

Study abroad. Any arrangement by which a student completes part of the college program—typically the junior year but sometimes only a semester or a summer—studying in another country. A college may operate a campus abroad, or it may have a cooperative agreement with some other American college or an institution of the other country.

Supplemental Educational Opportunity Grant Program (SEOG). A federal program administered by colleges that provides assistance for undergraduate students on the basis of need. For the current amount of the grants see the U.S. Department of Education booklet *Five Federal Financial Aid Program.* You can get a copy by calling toll free 800-638-6700.

Suspension. A sanction imposed for violation of disciplinary regulations. The student is separated from the university for a specified period of time. Permanent notification will appear on the student's transcript. The student shall not participate in any college or university sponsored activity and may be barred from the campus. Suspension usually requires administrative review.

Tenure. Status held by a teacher, which means that he can be dismissed only for adequate cause. Formal procedure is usually required to terminate.

Terminal program. An education program designed to prepare students for immediate employment. These programs usually can be completed in less than four years beyond high school and are available in many junior colleges, community colleges, and vocational-technical institutes.

Test of English as a Foreign Language (TOEFL). Sponsored by the College Board and the Graduate Record Examinations Board, this test helps foreign students demonstrate their English-language proficiency at the advanced level required for study in colleges and universities in the United States. Many colleges require their foreign applicants to take the test as part of their admissions requirements for both the undergraduate and graduate levels.

Tests of General Educational Development (GED). A series of five tests that adults who did not complete high school may take through their state education system to qualify for a high school equivalency certificate. The tests are also administered at centers outside the United States and to members of the armed services through the United States Armed Forces Institute.

3-2 liberal arts and career combination. A program in which a student completes three years of study in a liberal arts field followed by two years of professional/technical study (for example, engineering, allied health, forestry), at the end of which the student is awarded the bachelor of arts and bachelor of science degrees.

Transfer program. An education program in a two-year college that is offered primarily for students who plan to continue their studies in a four-year college or university.

Trimester. An academic calendar period of about 15 weeks. Three trimesters make up one year. Students make normal progress by attending two of the trimesters each year and in some colleges can accelerate their programs by attending all three trimesters in one or more years.

Trustees. Board of Directors of a private college or university.

Tuition. Cost of instruction, usually based on the academic year. May or may not include activities fees.

University. An educational institution that includes an undergraduate college, a graduate division and one or more professional schools such as law, medicine or engineering.

Undergraduate. Education at level of the four-year college. The first step above high school.

Upper-division college. A college offering bachelor's degree programs that begin with the junior year. Entering students must have completed the freshman and sophomore years at other colleges.

Upward Bound Program. Provides academic and counseling assistance to capable but underachieving high school students with the purpose of preparing them for some form of post-secondary education.

Vocational-technical program. An education program in a two-year college to prepare students for careers below the technical level produced in more advanced programs.

Work-study program. An arrangement by which the student combines employment and college study. The employment may be an integral part of the academic program (as in cooperative education or internships) or simply a means of paying for college (as in the College Work-Study Program).

APPENDIX B

ABBREVIATIONS COMMONLY USED IN COLLEGE AND UNIVERSITY CATALOGUES

A.A. — Associate in Arts Degree
ACE — American Council On Education
ACH — Achievement Tests
ACT — American College Testing Program
APP — Advanced Placement Program
A.S. — Associate in Science Degree
ATP — Admissions Testing Program
B.A. — Bachelor of Arts degree
BEOG — Basic Educational Opportunity Program
B.S. — Bachelor of Science degree
CAEL — Cooperative Assessment of Experimental Learning
CEEB — College Entrance Examination Board
CGP — Cooperative Guidance and Placement Program
CIEE — Council on International Education
CLEP — College Level Examination Program
CPEP — College Proficiency Examinations Program
CRDA — Candidates Replay Date Agreement
CSS — College Scholarship Service
CW-S — College Work-Study program
CWSP — College Work-Study program
DTLS/DTMS — Descriptive Tests of Language and Mathematics Skills
EDP-F/EDP-S — Early Decision Plan First and Second Choice
EEEO — Equal Education and Opportunity Officer
ETS — Educational Testing Service
FAF — Financial Aid Form
FFS — Family Financial Statement
FMCD — Family and Community Development Courses
GED — General Educational Development tests
GSL — Guaranteed Student Loan program
IED — Intensive Educational Development program
M.A. — Master of Arts degree
NASSGP — National Association of State Scholarship and Grant programs
NDSL — National Direct Student Loan program
NECAA — National Entertainment and Campus Activities Association
NMSQT — National Merit Scholarship Qualifying Test
NSA — National Student Association

NSEF — National Student Education Fund
NUEA — National University Extension Association
OEC — Office on Educational Credit
PCS — Parents Confidential Statement
Ph.D. — Doctor of Philosophy Degree
PEP — Proficiency Examination Program
PHEAA — Pennsylvania Higher Education Assistance Agency
PIRGS — Public Interest Research Group
PSAT — Preliminary Scholastic Aptitude Test
QPs — Quality points
REDE — Regents External Degree Program
SAAC — Student Aid Application for California
SAT — Scholastic Aptitude Test
SDQ — Student Descriptive Questionnaire
SEOG — Supplenmental Educational Opportunity Grant
SER — Student Eligibility Report
SGA — Student Government Association
SS# — Social Security number
TOEFL — Test of English as a Foreign Language
UGL — Undergraduate library
USAFI — United States Armed Forces Institute

APPENDIX C

The Institute of International Education (IIE) has updated bibliographical listings, new basic information on study in United States colleges and universities and a basic fact sheet on foreign study, all of which are available free to anyone who asks. Just write to:

Communications Division
Institute of International Education
809 United Nations Plaza
New York, NY 10017

The IIE, a nonprofit organization, is the oldest and largest international educational exchange agency in the United States. It has headquarters in New York City and a Washington, D.C. office; regional offices in Atlanta, Chicago, Denver, Houston and San Francisco; and overseas offices in Hong Kong, Bangkok and Mexico City.

NOTES

Chapter 1
1. Michael Edelhart, *College Knowledge*, Garden City, NY: Anchor Press/Doubleday, 1979.

Chapter 2
1. If you are looking for a program which is not offered at your community college, get the book *Guide to Two Year College Majors and Careers*, Chronicle Guidance Publications, Moravia, NY 13118 ($5.50).
2. *College Knowledge* offers more information on this subject on pages 343-347. It lists more sources of information and some words of wisdom for those interested in study abroad.
3. For more information on these new forms of higher education, see *College Knowledge*, pages 340-342.
4. Asa S. Knowles, *Handbook of College and University Administration*, New York: McGraw-Hill, 1970, p. 6
5. Ibid., p. 8.
6. Ibid., p. 24
7. Tim Walters and Al Siebert, *Student Success*, New York: Hold, Rinehart and Winston, 1971, 160 pp.

Chapter 3
1. Lewis B. Mayhew, *Surviving the Eighties*, San Francisco: Jossey-Bass, 1979, pp. 159, 160.
2. Ibid., p. 155.
3. Ibid.
4. Ibid., p. 156.
5. Ibid., pp. 157-160.
6. Ibid., p. 160.
7. Ibid., p. 95.
8. Ibid.
9. In addition to what I've offered already, let me recommend a nifty little booklet called *Choosing a College* by Patrick L. Miller (Downers Grove, IL: Inter-Varsity Press, 1979, 43 pp.).

1. The U.S. Department of Education publishes a useful fact sheet called *Five Federal Financial Aid Programs*. It is available through Financial Student Aid, P.O. Box 84, Washington, D.C. 20033, or you can call 202-472-5080 for a copy. Order this booklet today. You will need to understand the programs thoroughly to apply for aid. Don't be confused by some reference material referring to the Department of Health, Education and Welfare (HEW). Education is now a separate department.
2. *College Knowledge*, pp. 128-131.
3. K. Michael Ayers and Lee Hardy, *Need A Lift?* Indianapolis, IN: The American Legion, 1971.

4. Rexford G. Moon, Jr. and James E. Nelson, *Paying For Your Education*, The College Entrance Examination Board, New York, 1970, 63 pp.
5. Ibid., pp. 36-39.
6. When you work on the applications, photocopy them for a "dry run," and fill the copies in with a pencil, making any necessary changes as you go. When you have finished, use a pen and copy the information onto the originals for the final draft. If you cannot make photocopies, fill the originals in lightly with pencil so you can erase your mistakes. Fill them in with pen when you are sure you have them right.
7. For more information on RED, write the New York State Department of Education, Room 1919, 99 Washington Avenue, Albany, New York 12230.

Chapter 5
1. Mildred Z. Ward, *Introduction to Dorm Living*, Allentown, PA: Log Cabin Publishers, 1978, 18 pp.
2. See pages 62-116.
3. Available from Health Education Office, University of Maryland, College Park, MD 20742.

Chapter 6
1. Charles Hodge, *Systematic Theology*, 3 vols., Grand Rapids, MI: William B. Eerdmans Publishing Company, 1960, 2:263.
2. Cornelius Van Til, *Essays on Christian Education*, Phillipsburg, NJ: Presbyterian and Reformed Publishing Co., 1979, pp. 87, 88.
3. In the appendix you will find a reading list that will guide you to books on these subjects.

Chapter 7
1. Joseph Sobran, "Who's Who on Humanism Hill," *Eternity*, January 1982, p. 19. Used by permission.
2. *Time*, "The Man In the Water," January 25, 1982, p. 86.
3. J. I. Packer, *Knowing Man*, Westchester, IL: Cornerstone Books, 1979, p. 11.

4. Ranald Macaulay and Jerram Barrs, *Being Human: The Nature of Spiritual Experience*, Downers Grove, IL: Inter-Varsity Press, 1978, p. 15.
5. Fritz Ridenour, *How to Be a Christian in an Unchristian World*, Ventura, CA: Regal Books Division, Gospel Light Publications, 1971, pp. 65-68.
6. Donald G. Bloesch, "Secular Humanism—Not the Only Enemy," *Eternity*, January 1982, p. 22. Used by permission.

Chapter 8
1. A. W. Tozer, *The Christian Book of Mystical Verse*, Harrisburg, PA: Christian Publications, Inc., 1963, pp. 51-52.
2. Ibid., p. vi.
3. Ibid., p. 111.
4. Rousas John Rushdoony, *The Flight From Humanity*, Fairfax, VA: Thoburn Press, 1978, p. 1. Used by permission.
5. Ibid., p. 23.
6. ibid.
7. Ibid., p. 35.
8. Ibid., p. 37.

Chapter 9
1. For the female student and her parents who are security-minded, two of my monographs may be of interest: "What you Need to Know About Forcible Rape," and "What You Need to Know About Abusive or Obscene Phone Calls." Both the male and female student may want a third monograph, "More Information on VD." For the three monographs send $1.00 to Monographs, 12018 Long Ridge Lane, Bowie, MD 20715. For the VD monograph only, send 40¢.
2. Richard Hamilton, "Lovesick: the Terrible Curse of Herpes," *Rolling Stone*, March 4, 1982, p. 24.
3. *University of Maryland Undergraduate Catalogue 1981-1982*, University of Maryland at College Park, p. 10.

Chapter 10
1. For more information about Probe's ministry, write Probe Ministries, 12011 Coit Road, Suite 107, Dallas, TX 75251.